TEACH YOURSELF BOOKS

COMPOSE MUSIC

The few valuable books on musical composition that already exist treat their subject from a professional standpoint, assuming a working knowledge of harmony, form and other material, and are therefore of little use to the beginner. This book is an attempt to provide an introduction to composition simple enough to be grasped by any promising amateur who understands the rudiments of music.

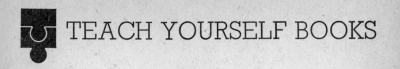

TEACH YOURSELF BOOKS

COMPOSE MUSIC

King Palmer

Associate of the Royal Academy of Music

ST. PAUL'S HOUSE WARWICK LANE LONDON EC4P 4AH

First printed 1947
Second edition 1972
Second impression 1974

Copyright © 1972
The English Universities Press Ltd.

ISBN 0 340 05552 9

Printed and bound in England
for The English Universities Press Ltd
by Hazell Watson & Viney Ltd, Aylesbury

PREFACE

Cookery and musical composition have little in common, yet both are included in this series under the general title "Teach Yourself". It is important, therefore, to draw some distinction between them lest the enthusiastic but unmusical reader should imagine that a piece of music can be produced as easily as an omelette. For whereas the cook has all the necessary ingredients to hand the composer must invent his material. Almost anyone can learn to cook, but only those with some degree of creative talent can hope to compose music.

The few valuable books on musical composition which already exist treat their subject from a professional standpoint, assuming a working knowledge of harmony, form, and other material, and are therefore of little use to the beginner. This book is an attempt to provide an introduction to composition simple enough to be grasped by any promising amateur who understands the rudiments of music.

During some thirty-five years as a musical editor many hundreds of compositions have passed through my hands. Many of these are frankly hopeless; others show that although their writers have some gift for melody they are at a loss to know how to handle their melodic and harmonic material. I hope that this book will be of value to those who have ideas, but who have hitherto struggled unaided to express them.

K. P.

TO MY PARENTS
IN GRATITUDE FOR
SO MUCH

CONTENTS

ACKNOWLEDGMENTS

The author's acknowledgments are gratefully made to Messrs. Chappell & Co., Ltd., for permission to print an extract from Sullivan's *Iolanthe ;* to Messrs. Novello & Co., Ltd. for extracts from German's *Henry VIII Dances;* to Messrs. W. Paxton & Co., Ltd., for an extract from Howard Carr's *The Carnival of the Elements.*

GENERAL PRINCIPLES OF MUSICAL COMPOSITION

The Equipment of the Composer

To the man in the street the art of the composer is something of a mystery. Though he may grasp the broad principles of painting, sculpture, or architecture, the processes of musical composition remain obscure. Even those who know enough about music to play the piano, or sing at sight, often have little or no idea how the composer goes to work.

Composition literally means " putting together," and the composer's art consists in putting musical sounds together in such a way that the result is a complete and well-balanced piece of music. This power of originating musical ideas, and of forming them into a sound musical structure, is a natural gift which cannot be imparted by books, or indeed, taught at all. The creation of the highest forms of music, such as the symphony or the string quartet, demands a degree of intellectual talent which may well amount to genius. These forms are outside the scope of this book, which is designed for the amateur who, though he cannot hope to scale the heights of the musical Parnassus, may find in the composition of the more modest forms of music a new and enthralling pursuit.

Often the wish to compose first asserts itself in the little scraps of melody which come into the head of the would-be composer. Usually the wish is thwarted through inability to develop these scraps into a complete melody, and to commit it to paper. The study of composition will encourage and develop this gift of melody, though it cannot, of course, act as a substitute for it. It is scarcely necessary to say that no amount of study will teach an unmusical man to write an original melody.

The origination of melody has been called " the true act of musical composition," and it is certain that without melody no real music can be said to exist ; but apart from the inspirational or " æsthetic " side, composition is a constructive art. " Music," says Hegel, " is Architecture translated from space into time—for in music, besides the deepest feeling, there is also a vigorous mathematical intelligence." It is not always realised that conscious labour is required, even in the construction of the simplest musical forms. This constructional skill, which constitutes the technique of composition, is only to be acquired by study and experience. It is an essential part of the composer's equipment, for without a sure technique, inspiration will remain an unruly, ill-disciplined talent.

Invention and Technique

The creative and constructional elements of composition may conveniently be labelled Invention and Technique.

Invention—the making of something new—is a mysterious process for which no rules can be formulated. No one can hope to invent who has not in him some spark of creative ability ; but this spark cannot burst into flame until an attempt is made to kindle it. Careful and thorough study, and painstaking experiment, are the only means by which any composer, however talented, can hope to produce music of artistic merit.

Creative talent is largely developed by a process of imitation. The artist, or the sculptor, at first directs his efforts towards the copying of familiar objects ; but as he progresses, unless he is content to remain a mere copyist, his work becomes less and less dependent on that of others, until at length it may justly be described as original. The beginner in composition must also have a model to guide him, and he should not be discouraged if his first attempts lack originality. As soon as the necessary experience is gained originality will begin to assert itself.

I am not for a moment suggesting that you should deliberately copy the style and mannerisms of any particular composer—such slavish imitation would lead to anything but originality—but simply that by listening intelligently to all the good music you are able to hear,[1] you may hope to gain an insight into the methods of composers of acknowledged skill. The wider your tastes the greater the benefit you are likely to reap ; the only stipulation is that whatever music you listen to shall be the best of its kind, whether symphony or ballad, opera or jazz.

The advice which Sir Joshua Reynolds once gave to students of art might well have been addressed to every budding composer : " The more extensive, therefore, your acquaintance is with the works of those who have excelled, the more extensive will be your powers of invention—and what may appear still more like a paradox, the more original will be your conceptions."

Technique—by which the composer builds his ideas into a sound musical structure—may be acquired through the study of the different branches of musical writing ; melody, harmony, rhythm, and so on. And since no constructive work is possible without a pre-conceived plan, the different forms in which music may be composed must also be studied.

---

[1] The radio and the gramophone bring to the composer of to-day invaluable opportunities of listening to music.

The Formation of Taste and Style

Style may be defined as the way in which ideas are expressed. Though style gives " finish " to a composition, it is not a concrete quality ; by this I mean that it cannot be separated from the ideas themselves. The beginner, though naturally anxious to form a style of his own, must be patient, for style is the outcome of taste, and the formation of taste cannot be hurried. The inexperienced composer must make certain of the quality of his ideas before he concerns himself with their treatment. " He who has nothing to assert," says Shaw, " has no style and can have none."

The only possible standard by which music can be judged is the standard of taste. That is why taste is an essential attribute of the composer. Taste is a word with more than one meaning, but I use it here in the sense of judgment, that is, the ability to tell good from bad. Now it is obvious that taste is personal, and that what you may consider good someone else may consider bad. There is no absolute test of goodness or badness ; even experienced critics, whose tastes one might suppose to be fully formed, are by no means always unanimous in their judgments. How then are you to form your musical taste ?

Fortunately there is a very simple solution. Whenever you are uncertain in your own judgment you may ask : What is the judgment of time ? Time has still to pass judgment on modern works, and it is difficult to choose with certainty among them. So you must turn first to the classics. I use " classic " in its widest sense— any work of acknowledged excellence ; that is, any work which has passed the test of time. Let us pick a few classics at random : Beethoven's 5th Symphony ; Sousa's *Washington Post* March ; Tschaikowsky's *Nut-*

cracker Suite ; Strauss' *Blue Danube* Waltzes. To choose a classic is to accept the judgment of past and present generations, a judgment formed over a period of half a century or more.

I do not for a moment suggest that every classic is a masterpiece by virtue of its being a classic ; but I do strongly suggest that any work that has passed the test of time is worthy of study, if only to find the reason for its survival. Arnold Bennett, in his " Literary Taste " (published by Jonathan Cape), an admirable book which, though written for literary aspirants, should be read by every composer, puts the matter thus : " If you differ with a classic it is you who are wrong, and not the book. If you differ with a modern work, you may be wrong or you may be right ; but no judge is authoritative enough to decide."

It must be remembered that the forms of composition treated of in this book have not undergone any radical changes during the last century or so. Modern composers of serious music are constantly seeking new idioms in which to express their ideas, but composers of light music are content to use pretty much the same idioms which served their grandfathers, adding a few modern trimmings here and there. This is because the first essential of light music is tunefulness, whereas in music of the " ultra-modern " school the tune is often presented in a form which is unfamiliar, and therefore incomprehensible, to the average listener.

Inspiration

At some time or other every composer experiences flashes of inspiration. They may visit him only a few times in his career, or they may come quite frequently. But it is safe to say that the average composer seldom has the time or the patience to sit down and wait for inspiration before he puts pen to paper. Experience soon teaches him that precious little comes to him who waits.

If inspiration could be turned on and off at will, as easily as a tap, the composer would never find himself at a loss for ideas. As things are he is often obliged to compose at the very time when his stock of inventive talent seems to have run out—in the film and theatre world, in particular, music is frequently commissioned at very short notice. Much of this music seems none the worse for having been written under compulsion. Some composers even assert that pressure of time stimulates the flow of their ideas ; Rossini, who once advised a young composer not to write the overture to his opera until the day before the first performance, certainly believed that necessity is the mother of invention.

The advice once given to would-be composers to buy pen and paper and start to compose is not so unhelpful as it appears to be. It is a timely reminder that in order to swim you must first enter the water. I am taking it for granted that before attempting the actual act of composition you will have acquired sufficient technique to enable you to put your ideas on paper. This much accomplished, the next step is to set aside definite periods for composing, and during those periods, instead of waiting like Micawber for " something to turn up," to make a start with the best of the ideas that happen to present themselves.

Professional composers usually work to some sort of timetable—one well-known composer always starts work after breakfast and continues until tea-time ; another finds that his most productive period is in the evening. The amateur should try to arrange matters so that he can devote one or more regular periods during the week to composition. These periods should be as long as possible ; one three-hour period is of greater value than three one-hour periods. For this there is sound reason. The composer is not in the position of the bricklayer, who can pick up his tools and continue where he left off. The composer has to spend some time getting down to his work—his brain, like an engine on a frosty morning, must be warmed up before it can function properly. Once this warming up process is completed his ideas will begin to flow more freely, and continue to flow until the trend of his thoughts is again interrupted.

Almost every composer experiences the difficulty of making a start. Schubert is a notable exception ; ideas seemed to come to him entirely without effort. " I compose every morning," he once said, " and as soon as one piece is finished I begin another." Lesser mortals must find some means of bringing their recalcitrant ideas to life. Three different methods may be proposed, and these in turn may suggest others, but only you yourself can decide which method, or combination of methods, you ought to adopt.

(1) *The piano may be used as an aid to composition.* Rimsky-Korsakoff recommended the practice of working out ideas at the piano to his pupils ; Schumann condemned it in these words : " When you begin to compose, do it all with your brain. Do not try the piece until it is finished." But it is probable that most modern composers use the piano, either to discover ideas or to test their value when they have been found. Most of the great composers were pianists or organists ; some excelled in extemporization (the art of composing music at the keyboard) which often helped them to create ideas for

their works. A few, like Berlioz, could not play the piano.

You may or may not be a pianist. If you are not you must at least teach yourself to pick out printed music on the keyboard (it does not matter how slowly) so that you will be able to play the musical examples in this book, and to experiment with chords and progressions. (Anyone who knows the rudiments of music can gain this knowledge in a few weeks by studying the chapters on piano-playing in the companion volume to this book, " Teach Yourself Music "). Only the experienced composer is able to receive mental impressions of sounds before he hears them played ; and although this is the ultimate goal of the beginner he must learn to hear with his ears before he can hear with his mind.

When you begin, then, you will find it best to work at the piano, and perhaps, like Wagner, you will fit some kind of desk over the keyboard (a stout sheet of cardboard placed on the music desk will do) so that you can jot down your ideas as they come to you. Your search for ideas should be something more than a blind groping at the keyboard in the hope of discovering something worth developing ; it should take the form of the experimental building up of melodies and chord progressions. Even the playing of a succession of simple chords may give rise to ideas.

In literature there are certain plots which belong not to an individual but to the world—the Cinderella story, for example—and these have been used by countless writers who have so transformed them that they appear surprisingly fresh and original. In music, also, certain passages and combinations may be regarded as common property, and these ideas (with others newly invented) may be employed in such a way as to exhibit them in a new light. Some of the most original ideas often arise out of unoriginal material.

2. *You may keep a sketch book.* The practice of keeping a small music book, in which fragments of melody, or other ideas, may be jotted down, has obvious advantages. Every composer knows that good ideas sometimes present themselves at inconvenient moments —on the top of a bus, or in the middle of the night. If a sketch book is carried these fleeting hints of tunes may be preserved, and will form a stock of ideas for the composer to draw on when inspiration fails him. Beethoven in his boyhood, realizing that ideas are evanescent—at one moment crystal clear, at the next gone for ever—was never without his sketch book. The sketches in Beethoven's note books were usually hasty jottings intended to assist the memory, and he would revise and polish them with unremitting care before he made use of them in his compositions. Schubert, whose invention was so fertile that he needed no sketch book, is said to have slept in his spectacles with pen and paper beside him, so that he could immediately record his ideas when he awoke. Sullivan used a sketch book, and many of the melodies which he jotted down at odd moments eventually found their way into his comic operas.

3. *You may seek inspiration by listening to the music of other composers.* Several well-known composers have used this method. César Franck played the music of Wagner on the piano to stimulate his ideas. And many composers of popular music find that one melody suggests another. Sometimes, of course, such ideas come by accident instead of by design ; music from a neighbour's radio set or a passing military band has been known to inspire the composition of some piece or other. But where ideas are deliberately courted you must choose

suitable music ; if you want to write a march or a waltz you must listen to martial or " waltzy " music, and not to the slow movement of a symphony. The purpose is not so much to give you ideas as to put you in sympathy with your subject so that ideas will come more easily. A composer writes " melting airs, or martial, brisk or grave " according to his mood, and the stronger the mood, even if it is artificially created by listening to other composers' music, the greater the chances of success.

Making a Start

The chapters of this book are arranged in the order in which they should be studied. The amount of time which ought to be devoted to each chapter depends largely on the aptitude of the student, and the extent of his musical experience. The average beginner who has no knowledge of harmony, and who can devote only a few hours a week to the study of musical composition, should spend at least a year over the ground covered by this book. In spite of a natural desire to begin creative work at the earliest possible moment, I would urge the would-be composer not to hurry over the preliminary chapters. The principles outlined in these chapters provide the material of composition, and the beginner should not attempt to build until he is satisfied with the quality of his material. The exercises which accompany each chapter should be worked, and re-worked, until the difficulties which are bound to arise are surmounted.

A number of musical examples are included in the text, and these must be carefully played on the piano so that the mental effect of each progression is appreciated. The examples should be supplemented by reference to similar examples which are to be found in printed music. In studying chord progressions a book of hymn tunes will be found particularly useful.

Finally, it must be emphasized that even the most talented composer must be prepared to face much painstaking labour (some of which is frankly dull) before he can hope to produce music of real merit. Even though the amateur may wisely limit his efforts to the composition of the more simple forms, he must set himself a professional standard of competence, for only such a standard will bring from him his utmost endeavours. Composition, after all, is an art, not a pastime for dabblers.

CHAPTER II

SCALES AND INTERVALS

I assume that you already understand the rudiments of musical notation—the names of the notes, clefs, time signatures, and so on. Without this knowledge it is impossible to play the piano from printed music, and equally impossible to compose, unless one follows the example of the " tin pan alley " composers (sometimes called " tunesmiths "), who hum over their tunes to somebody who is capable of putting them on paper and harmonizing them. About this particular talent, which is said to bring fame and fortune to many of its possessors, I can offer no useful advice.

Strictly speaking, scales and intervals should be included in the rudiments of music, but their study is usually neglected by amateurs, and even those who know something about them will do well to refresh their memories.

Semitones and Tones

If you play two different notes on the piano, it is obvious that one must be the higher note, and the other the lower. The distance, or difference of pitch, between the two sounds is called an **Interval**. In theory there is no limit to the size of an interval—the top and bottom notes of the piano, for instance, might form one huge interval. But in practice only a small number of intervals need be considered.

The smallest interval in modern music is called a **Semitone** (or half-tone)—on the piano this is the distance from one note to the note immediately above or below it ; the semitone above C, for instance, is C sharp, and that below C is B natural. Two semitones make a **Tone** (or whole-tone)—the tone above C, for instance, is D, and that below C is B flat. Example I shows a section of the piano keyboard. You will see that between the white keys E and F, and B and C, there is no black key ; they are therefore a semitone apart. On the other hand, the white keys C and D, D and E, F and G, G and A, have a black key between them, and are therefore a tone apart.

EXAMPLE 1

You may have noticed that there are two kinds of semitones ; the notes forming the first kind have different letter names (B to C, E to F, and so on), and the notes forming the second kind have the same letter name (C to C sharp, D to D sharp, and so on). A glance at the diagram of the piano keyboard will make this clear.

If we put these two kinds of semitones into musical notation you will notice another difference.

EXAMPLE 2

You will see that the notes marked (*a*) are on two different positions of the stave (C on a space, B on a line), and that the notes marked (*b*) are both on the same position of the stave, the second note (C sharp) being altered by the addition of an accidental. The name given to the first kind of semitone (*a*) is **Diatonic,** a word meaning " through the tones, or degrees, of the scale." The name given to the second kind of semitone (*b*) is **Chromatic,** which literally means " coloured " ; in a figurative sense a note may be looked upon as being coloured when it is raised or lowered by means of an accidental.

The difference may be summarized thus :

The notes of a Diatonic Semitone have different letter names, and are on two different positions of the stave.

The notes of a Chromatic Semitone have the same letter name, and are both on the same position of the stave.

The Formation of Scales

A simple definition of **a Scale** is a ladder of notes arranged in alphabetical order. We may, of course, either ascend or descend the ladder. There are two principal kinds of scales, and like the two kinds of semitones they take the names of Diatonic and Chromatic.

A Diatonic Scale consists of seven different notes arranged in alphabetical order. There are two varieties of Diatonic Scales (Major and Minor), but before we consider their differences let us see what they have in common.

EXAMPLE 3

SCALE OF C MAJOR

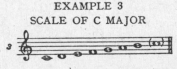

It will be seen that each note of the scale is placed on a different space or line of the stave. If the scale is continued beyond the seventh note, the eighth note will be a repetition of the first note at a different pitch, and will have the same letter name. This eighth note is said to be the **Octave** (abbreviated **8ve**) of the first note. Similarly the ninth note of the scale is the octave of the second note, and so on. A moment's thought will show that the fifteenth note of the scale is two octaves above the first note, and so on. Although the Diatonic Scale is made up of only seven *different* notes, the ear does not recognize it as complete until the eighth note (the Octave) is added. If you will play the first seven notes of the scale you will notice the strong tendency of the seventh note to lead upwards to the Octave.

The Major Scale

We must now consider the different characteristics of the Major and Minor forms of the Diatonic Scale. The **Major Scale** is made up of tones and semitones, and these are arranged according to a definite plan ; namely, semitones occur between the third and fourth, and seventh and eighth notes, and tones between the other notes.

EXAMPLE 4

SCALE OF C MAJOR

From the example above you will see that the Major Scale may be divided into two halves, one half consisting of the first four notes, and the other of the last four notes. Each half is called a **Tetrachord** (a Greek word originally applied to the four strings of the lyre), and each will be seen to consist of precisely similar intervals—two tones followed by one semitone. The two tetrachords are separated by the interval of a tone.

Every Major Scale is constructed according to this pattern. We may take the *upper* tetrachord of the scale of C major, and make it the *lower* tetrachord of an entirely new scale, adding another tetrachord above it.

EXAMPLE 5

SCALE OF G MAJOR

You will see that the first note (also called the **Key-note**) of the new scale is G ; that is, the fifth note of the scale of C Major. To make the upper tetrachord conform to the regular pattern of two tones followed by one semitone, the third note of the tetrachord (*i.e.* the seventh note of the scale) must be raised a semitone.

In the scale of G Major (which takes its name from the key-note, G), therefore, the seventh note (F) is sharpened. As this sharp is obviously vital to the construction of the scale, it is placed at the beginning of the stave, immediately after the clef sign, and is known as the **key-signature**.[1] A key-signature may consist of either sharps or flats (from one to seven), and these are known as **essentials** because they affect every note of the same letter name throughout the movement.

---

[1] The key-note of a scale also lends its name to the **Key** of the music. The key indicates the scale system upon which a composition is constructed ; if, for example, the notes forming the scale of G Major are chosen as the main material for a composition, the music is said to be in the key of G Major, and is given a key-signature of one sharp.

Thus they differ from **accidentals,** which are signs of
sharpening or flattening, affecting notes of the same
letter name and in the same octave, only in the actual
bar in which they occur. If, for example, the key-
signature in Example 6 were to be replaced by ac-

EXAMPLE 6

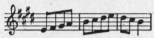

cidentals, the passage would have to be written thus :

EXAMPLE 7

Six sharps in the second example against four in
the first ! The object of a key-signature, then, is to
reduce the number of accidentals.

Now let us return to the formation of scales. If we
make the upper tetrachord of the scale of G Major into
the lower tetrachord of a new scale, and add another
tetrachord above it, we form the scale of D Major.
(Notice that the key-note is again the fifth note of the
old scale.)

EXAMPLE 8
SCALE OF D MAJOR

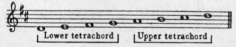

To make the upper tetrachord conform to pattern
we must raise the seventh note of the scale a semitone,
by adding another sharp to the key-signature.

By continuing the process of making the fifth note
of one scale into the key-note of another, we may form,
successively, the major scales of A, E, B, F sharp, and

C sharp. Each time the seventh note of the scale must be raised a semitone by adding another sharp to the key-signature.

EXAMPLE 9

SCALE OF A MAJOR   SCALE OF E MAJOR

SCALE OF B MAJOR   SCALE OF F Sharp MAJOR

SCALE OF C Sharp MAJOR

It is possible to continue the process still further, and to form the scales of G sharp Major, D sharp Major, and so on, but these scales necessitate the use of eight or more sharps in the key-signature, and they are therefore never used for practical purposes.

We must now turn our attention to that series of Major Scales which has one or more flats in the key-signature. Again we start with the scale of C Major. (It is helpful to think of this as the Natural Major Scale, since it can be played on the piano entirely on the white, or natural, keys.) But this time we reverse the process; we take the *lower* tetrachord and make it into the *upper* tetrachord of the new scale, adding another tetrachord *below* it.

EXAMPLE 10

SCALE OF F MAJOR

Two points should be noticed : (*a*) the key-note of the old scale now becomes the fifth note of the new scale ; (*b*) in order to obtain a semitone between the third and fourth notes, and a tone between the two tetrachords, the fourth note must be lowered a semitone, by giving the scale a key-signature of one flat.

By continuing this process we may form, successively, the Major Scales of B flat, E flat, A flat, D flat, G flat, and C flat. Each time the fourth note of the new scale must be lowered by adding another flat to the key-signature.

EXAMPLE 11

SCALE OF B FLAT MAJOR   SCALE OF E FLAT MAJOR

SCALE OF A FLAT MAJOR   SCALE OF D FLAT MAJOR

SCALE OF G FLAT MAJOR   SCALE OF C FLAT MAJOR

Again it is possible to continue the process, and to form the scales of F flat Major, B double flat Major, and so on, but these scales necessitate the use of eight or more flats in the key-signature, and are never used for practical purposes.

But we may use such keys as G sharp Major and F flat Major, if we convert them into other forms. We know that on the piano G sharp is the same note as A flat. We can therefore change the key of G sharp Major into the key of A flat Major, and though the notation will be different the effect will be precisely the same. Similarly, we can convert F flat Major into

E Major, C flat Major into B Major, and so on. This conversion of sharp keys into flat keys, and vice versa, is known as an **Enharmonic Change.** The table below shows the enharmonic relation between the flat keys and the sharp keys—you should note it in passing, but you need not memorize it as we shall not be using enharmonics for the time being.

F Major is the Enharmonic of	E sharp Major
(1 flat)	(11 sharps)
B flat ,, ,, ,, ,, ,, A sharp Major	
(2 flats)	(10 sharps)
E flat ,, ,, ,, ,, ,, D sharp Major	
(3 flats)	(9 sharps)
A flat ,, ,, ,, ,, ,, G sharp Major	
(4 flats)	(8 sharps)
D flat ,, ,, ,, ,, ,, C sharp Major	
(5 flats)	(7 sharps)
G flat ,, ,, ,, ,, ,, F sharp Major	
(6 flats)	(6 sharps)
C flat ,, ,, ,, ,, ,, B Major	
(7 flats)	(5 sharps)
F flat ,, ,, ,, ,, ,, E Major	
(8 flats)	(4 sharps)

Reference to the table above will show that if the number of sharps in a key-signature is deducted from twelve, the result will be the number of flats in the key-signature of its Enharmonic, and vice versa. For example, the key-signature of D flat Major has five flats, and five from twelve leaves seven, which is the number of sharps in the key-signature of its Enharmonic, C sharp Major.

The Minor Scale

Though the Major Scale has remained unaltered for about two centuries, the Minor Scale has undergone

several changes.　The earliest form comes from the
scale system of the ancient Greeks, and is one of the old
Church scales or " modes "—the Aeolian.

EXAMPLE 12

SCALE OF A MINOR—Ancient Form

You will see that this scale is formed of natural notes
(*i.e.* it may be played on the white keys of the piano).
Its peculiarity is that there is an interval of a tone
between the seventh and eighth notes, whereas one of
the features of our modern scalic system is that these
notes are a semitone apart.　So in order to produce this
final semitone the Ancient form of the Minor Scale is
usually modified when it is used in modern music.　This
modification may be effected in two different ways.　The
most simple method is just to sharpen the seventh note
of the scale, and when this is done we form what is known
as the **Harmonic Minor Scale.**

EXAMPLE 13

SCALE OF A MINOR—Harmonic Form

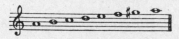

You will see that by sharpening the seventh note of
the scale the interval between the sixth and seventh
notes is raised a semitone, and is now a tone-and-a-half
This interval (we shall learn shortly that it is an augmented second) was forbidden in old music, which was
mostly written for voices, because it was considered
difficult to sing.　With the rise of instrumental music the

Harmonic Minor Scale found favour, and is now the form most used in modern music.

In order to overcome the objection to an interval of a tone-and-a-half between the sixth and seventh notes, the **Melodic Minor Scale** was evolved. This scale, as its name implies, is chiefly used in the construction of melody, whereas the principal use of the Harmonic Minor Scale is in the construction of chords—*i.e.* harmony.

The peculiarity of the Melodic Minor Scale is that it uses different forms in ascending and descending. The sixth and seventh notes of the scale are sharpened in ascending, but restored to their original pitch in descending.

EXAMPLE 14

SCALE OF A MINOR—Melodic Form

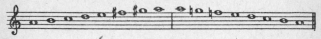

You will see that the semitones fall between the second and third, and seventh and eighth notes in ascending, but between the second and third, and fifth and sixth notes in descending. The descending form is, in fact, the same as that of the Ancient Minor Scale.

We have seen that the Ancient Scale of A Minor is formed of natural notes, and has no sharps or flats in the key-signature. Since the Harmonic and Melodic forms are evolved from this ancient scale, the seventh note in the Harmonic Scale, and the sixth and seventh notes in the Melodic Scale (ascending), are regarded as being **accidentally sharpened** ; this means that the sharps are used as accidentals, instead of being inserted in the key-signature. Similarly, the naturals in the Melodic Scale of A Minor (descending) are used as accidentals.

Since the Ancient Scale of A Minor and the scale of C Major are both formed from natural notes, and neither has sharps or flats in the key-signature, A Minor is spoken of as the Relative Minor of C Major, and C Major as the Relative Major of A Minor

A moment's thought will show that the sixth note of C Major is the key-note of A Minor ; the sixth note of any Major scale is, in fact, the key-note of its Relative Minor. Similarly, the third note of any Minor scale is the key-note of its Relative Major. From the Natural Scale of A Minor a series of Minor Scales may be constructed which is relative to the series of Major Scales formed from the Natural Scale of C Major.[1]

The process of forming Major Scales has already been described in detail, and much the same process applies to the formation of Minor Scales. To form the " sharp " series we take the upper tetrachord of a scale and add a tetrachord above it ; to form the " flat " series we take the lower tetrachord and add a tetrachord below it. Two important points, however, must be noticed. (1) The two tetrachords which form the Minor Scale are not

---

[1] The relationship of Relative Major and Minor Scales consists in their having more notes in common than any two Major and Minor scales which are not so related, and is shown by the two scales having the same key-signature. Apart from this relationship a Major Scale is totally distinct from its Relative Minor, both in derivation and effect. On the other hand, a Major Scale is closely allied to the Minor Scale having the same key-note. If the scales of C Major and C Minor are compared, they will be found to have five notes in common, including the key-note. A Minor Scale whose key-note is that of a Major Scale is said to be the **Tonic Minor** of that scale (Tonic, as we shall see, is another name for key-note), though it does not have the same key-signature. The Key-signature of a Minor Scale has three sharps less, or three flats more, than that of its Tonic Major : C sharp Major, for instance, has seven sharps, and C sharp Minor four ; E flat Major has three flats, and E flat Minor six.

identical in construction like those of the Major Scale ; when the lower tetrachord of one scale is made into the upper tetrachord of another, and vice versa, some modification is therefore necessary. (2) To form the Harmonic Minor Scale the seventh note must be accidentally sharpened ; to form the Melodic Minor Scale the sixth and seventh notes must be accidentally sharpened in ascending, and restored to their original pitch in descending.

To make this process clear let us take the upper tetrachord of the Ancient Scale of A Minor, and above it add a tetrachord consisting of a semitone, a tone, and a tone.

EXAMPLE 15

SCALE OF E MINOR—Ancient Form

This gives us the Ancient Scale of E Minor, and since E is the sixth note of G Major, the two scales are relative to one another, each having a key-signature of one sharp. This sharp has the effect of raising the second note of the scale a semitone. In other words, by adding a sharp to the key-signature we have modified the upper tetrachord of the old scale, A Minor, to make it conform to the pattern of the lower tetrachord of the new scale, E Minor.

Having formed the Ancient Scale of E Minor we may turn it into either the Harmonic or the Melodic form. In the Harmonic form the seventh note must be accidentally sharpened.

EXAMPLE 16
SCALE OF E MINOR—Harmonic Form

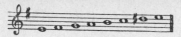

In the Melodic form the sixth and seventh notes must be accidentally sharpened in ascending, and restored to their original pitch in descending.

EXAMPLE 17
SCALE OF E MINOR—Melodic Form

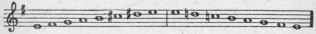

If these principles are grasped it is unnecessary to continue the process of forming the Minor Scales which have sharps in their key-signatures.

The " flat " series of Minor Scales is formed by taking the lower tetrachord of the Ancient Scale and adding a tetrachord below it (tone, semitone, tone).

EXAMPLE 18

SCALE OF D MINOR—Ancient Form

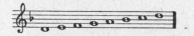

Since D is the sixth note of the scale of F Major, the scale of D Minor is relative to it, both scales having a key-signature of one flat. This flat has the effect of modifying the second tetrachord of the D Minor Scale, by lowering the sixth note a semitone.

The table below shows every Major Scale with its Relative Minor, and the key-signature which is common to both scales.

EXAMPLE 19

MAJOR, AND RELATIVE MINOR KEYS

The Chromatic Scale

The Chromatic Scale consists entirely of semitones ; that is, each note is a semitone's distance from the next one. There are twelve different notes in the Chromatic Scale, and these are arranged in alphabetical order, though there may be two notes of the same letter name ; C and C sharp, D and D sharp, and so on. If the scale is continued beyond the twelfth note, the thirteenth note will be a repetition of the first at a higher pitch, the fourteenth note a repetition of the second, and so on.

The Chromatic Scale is usually formed by taking the notes of the Major scale and filling in the missing semitones, sharpening the notes in ascending (by the addition of sharps or naturals), and flattening them in descending (by the addition of flats or naturals). The first two notes of the scale of C Major, for example, are C to D, a tone apart. In forming the Chromatic Scale we fill in the missing semitone by adding a sharpened C in ascending, and a flattened D in descending.

The example below will make this clear ; the white-headed notes are those of the Major Scale, and the black-headed notes those added to form the Chromatic Scale.

EXAMPLE 20
KEY OF C MAJOR

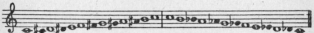

If the key-signature contains sharps or flats, the Chromatic Scale is formed in the same way (*i.e.* by taking the Major Scale and filling in the missing semitones), those notes which are sharpened or flattened by the key-signature remaining undisturbed.

EXAMPLE 21
KEY OF B Flat MAJOR

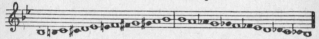

This method of writing the Chromatic Scale uses fewer accidentals than any other. If you re-write either of the examples, flattening the notes in ascending and sharpening them in descending, you will find that twice as many accidentals will be required—twenty instead of ten.

The Degrees of the Scale

In theory each note of the Diatonic Scale is called a **degree** ; the key-note is the first degree, the second note the second degree, and so on. Each degree is given a technical name,[1] and as these names are necessary to the

---

[1] In Tonic Sol-Fa notation a similar system of naming the degrees of the scale is used ; the key-note is named DOH, and the other degrees, in order, RAY, MI, FAH, SO, LAH, TE.

study of harmony, it is important that you should understand and memorize them. The degrees of the Diatonic Scale are always counted *upwards*—in the key of C the first degree is C, the second D, the third E, and so on.

The first degree, or **Key-note,** is known as the **Tonic.** This is the most important degree, and from it the scale (and therefore the key) takes its name. The principal key in which a piece of music is written is spoken of as the **Tonic Key.**

The second degree is the **Supertonic ;** *i.e.* the note above the Tonic.

The third degree is the **Mediant,** so-called because it occupies an intermediate position between the Tonic (first degree) and the Dominant (fifth degree).

The fourth degree is the **Subdominant ;** *i.e.* the note below the Dominant. This note ranks third in importance in the scale.

The fifth degree is the **Dominant.** This, as its name implies, is the " ruling " note of the scale, and is next in importance to the Tonic. You will see later that the chord formed on the Dominant plays a principal part in defining the key of the music.

The sixth degree is the **Submediant,** or lower Mediant, so-called because it is the same distance (three degrees) below the upper Tonic (eighth degree) as the Mediant is above the Tonic.

The seventh degree is the **Leading Note,** so-called because of its strong tendency to lead to the upper Tonic.

The eighth degree is, of course, a repetition of the first degree, an octave higher in pitch.

The table which follows may be useful for quick reference.

Degrees of the Diatonic Scale

1st degree.   **Tonic,** or **Key-note.**
2nd degree.   **Supertonic.**
3rd degree.   **Mediant.**
4th degree.   **Subdominant.**
5th degree.   **Dominant.**
6th degree.   **Submediant.**
7th degree.   **Leading Note.**
8th degree.   **Tonic,** or **Key-note.**

INTERVALS

We have seen that an interval is the distance between two sounds, and consists of an upper note and a lower note. The size of an interval may be calculated by counting the letter names *upwards*, from the lower note to the higher note, both notes being included in the total. The interval from C to D, for example, contains two letter names and is therefore a **second** ; that from C to E contains three letter names, and is therefore a **third,** and so on.

The sharpening or flattening of either or both the notes forming an interval does not alter its numerical name ; thus the intervals C flat to D, C to D, and C sharp to D are all seconds, though each differs in quality.

Any interval which is counted from the first note of a Major Scale to any other note of that scale is either a **perfect**[1] or a **major** interval.

EXAMPLE 22

| Major 2nd | Major 3rd | Perfect 4th | Perfect 5th | Major 6th | Major 7th | Perfect 8th |

(Octave)

[1] A perfect interval is so named because the ratio between the number of vibrations required to produce the lower sound and the upper sound is more or less perfect. Thus the ratio between the two sounds of the octave is 1 to 2, and that between the two sounds of the perfect fifth 2 to 3.

Though Example 22 shows the perfect and major intervals in the key of C Major, the rule of course applies to intervals in all Major keys.

In addition to the intervals of a perfect fourth, fifth and octave, the **unison,** which is formed by two notes of the same pitch and letter name, is spoken of as perfect, though strictly speaking it is not an interval at all. The unison is shown thus:

EXAMPLE 23

If a major interval (a second, third, sixth, or seventh) is reduced by a semitone, either by flattening the upper note or sharpening the lower note, it becomes a **minor** interval.

EXAMPLE 24

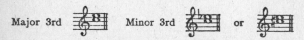

Major 3rd   Minor 3rd   or

If a perfect or a major interval is increased by a semitone, either by sharpening the upper note or flattening the lower note, it becomes an **augmented** interval.

EXAMPLE 25

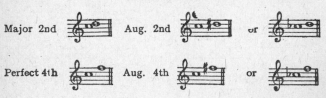

Major 2nd   Aug. 2nd   or

Perfect 4th   Aug. 4th   or

If a perfect or a minor interval is reduced by a semitone, either by flattening the upper note or by sharpening the lower note, it becomes a **diminished** interval.

EXAMPLE 26

The table below shows the different varieties of intervals, each of which has C natural for its lower note.

TABLE OF INTERVALS

(The figures in brackets show the number of semitones in each interval.)

Diminished	Minor	Major	Perfect	Augmented
Second				
C to D♭♭[1]	C to D♭ (1)	C to D (2)	——	C to D♯ (3)
Third				
C to E♭♭ (2)	C to E♭ (3)	C to E (4)	——	C to E♯ (5)
Fourth				
C to F♭ (4)	——	——	C to F (5)	C to F♯ (6)
Fifth				
C to G♭ (6)	——	——	C to G (7)	C to G♯ (8)
Sixth				
C to A♭♭ (7)	C to A♭ (8)	C to A (9)	——	C to A♯ (10)
Seventh				
C to B♭♭ (9)	C to B♭ (10)	C to B (11)	——	C to B♯[1] (12)
Eighth (Octave)				
C to C♭ (11)	——	——	C to C (12)	C to C♯ (13)

From this table you will see that (1) perfect intervals can be either augmented or diminished ; major intervals can be augmented but not diminished (if reduced by a

---

[1] The interval of a diminished second is, in effect, a unison, and that of an augmented seventh, an octave. These two intervals are only used when an enharmonic change is required. (*See* page 22.)

semitone they become minor) ; and minor intervals can be diminished but not augmented (if increased by a semitone they become major) ; (2) the interval of a minor second is the same as that of a diatonic semitone ; (3) some intervals contain the same number of semitones, but are differently named. Thus the interval C to G flat, which contains six semitones, is a fifth (diminished) because it includes five letter names, C, D, E, F, G ; whereas the interval C to F sharp, which also contains six semitones, is a fourth (augmented) because it includes only four letter names, C, D, E, F.

Compound Intervals

Intervals which do not exceed the compass of an octave are called **simple intervals** ; those which do exceed the compass of an octave are called **compound intervals.** A compound interval is a simple interval to which an octave has been added ; by subtracting seven a compound interval is reduced to a simple interval, and is then treated as if it were that interval. Thus a ninth is reduced to a second (9—7=2), and treated as such ; a tenth is reduced to a third (10—7=3), and so on. When a compound interval is reduced to a simple one the quality is unchanged—the compound equivalent of a minor third is a minor tenth, that of a perfect fifth is a perfect twelfth, and so on. The interval of a fifteenth is, of course, a compound octave, and is usually spoken of as a **double octave.**

Inverted Intervals

If the relative position of the two notes which form an interval is changed (*i.e.* if the lower note is placed above the upper one, or the upper note below the lower one) the interval is said to be **inverted.** Thus

when inverted becomes [music] or [music]   The sum of the letter names in any interval and its inversion is always nine, so that the number of the inversion is found by subtracting the uninverted interval from nine. Thus the interval C to G, which is a fifth, becomes a fourth when inverted (9—5=4).

Perfect intervals, when inverted, remain perfect, but major intervals become minor, minor become major, augmented become diminished, and diminished become augmented.

Consonance and Dissonance

Intervals which appeal to the ear as complete in themselves, and which do not require another sound to follow, are said to be **consonant.** Intervals which leave a sense of incompleteness, and a desire to resolve into some other sound, are said to be **dissonant.**

A major sixth, for example, gives an impression of completeness, and is therefore a consonant interval. An augmented fourth, on the other hand, leaves a sense of incompleteness until it is resolved into some other sound.

Play the two intervals in Example 27, and you will notice that the first (a dissonance) sounds incomplete until it is resolved into the second (a consonance), which gives an impression of completeness.

EXAMPLE 27

The intervals which are usually classed as consonant are all perfect intervals, and major and minor thirds and sixths : those classed as dissonant are major and minor seconds and sevenths, and all augmented and diminished intervals. This distinction, though generally recognized by theorists, is necessarily an arbitrary one, as what is accepted by one hearer as a dissonance may be regarded as a consonance by another.

Exercises

It is of the utmost importance that you should acquire the power of recognizing all the intervals of the Major and Minor Scale when you hear them played, and of hearing them mentally when you see them on paper. The following exercises should be persevered with until these results are obtained.

(1) Play the intervals of the Major and Minor Scale (in several different keys) on the piano, listening carefully to the characteristics of the different intervals so as to fix them in the mind. You will find it useful to invent a description of your own for each interval, according to its particular mental effect. Thus a third or a sixth might be thought of as rich or sweet, a fifth as open or bare, and so on.

(2) Write down various intervals in several different keys and play one note of each interval (either the upper or the lower) afterwards singing the other one. Then test for accuracy by playing the second note.

(3) Have various intervals played on the piano (*a*) giving the quality of each (*e.g.* major third, diminished fifth, and so on), and (*b*) writing down the interval from dictation, the Tonic of the key in which the interval occurs having been previously sounded and named.

CHAPTER III

FIRST STEPS IN MELODY MAKING

Modern music consists of three principal elements : melody, harmony, and rhythm.

Melody, broadly speaking, is a succession of single musical sounds arranged in an effective order.

Harmony is the science of combining sounds: *i.e.* chord building.

Rhythm is the element that imparts shape to melody and harmony, and moulds them into musical thoughts.

These three elements are so closely allied that it is difficult to think of them separately. A few melodies, including some of the old folk-tunes, are so attractive in themselves that they do not need to be supported by harmony. But modern melodies generally require the assistance of harmony of some sort ; indeed, many have their origin in the harmony that accompanies them. Harmony without melody is impossible ; the simplest progression of chords produces some kind of melody. And though rhythm may exist by itself (*e.g.* the beating of a drum, or the click of tap-dancing) neither melody nor harmony can exist without it.

When a composer invents a melody, therefore, he also invents the rhythm which gives it shape, and more often than not he forms a conscious or unconscious impression of the harmony.

Modern melody may be looked upon as the surface, or horizontal aspect, of harmony, and harmony as the depth, or vertical aspect, of melody. This explains the ease with which melody catches the ear (as a polished surface catches the eye), and the greater concentration necessary to penetrate the " depth " of harmony. It should not be thought, however, that melody is confined to the top part, or tune, of a piece of music. The bass, and the inner parts, must also be made as melodious as possible.

The Construction of Melody

Although the *invention* of melody cannot be taught it is quite possible to show how melody is constructed. In the first place it is obvious that a mere succession of sounds (*e.g.* a dozen notes played at random on the piano) does not constitute a melody. The first essential of a melody is that it shall be written in some definite key, and that the intervals of which it consists shall form part of some regular scale. Thus in every melody there is an implied key-note, or Tonic ; this is the note upon which so many tunes start and finish (*e.g. God Save the Queen, Home Sweet Home, All Through the Night*). When we come to the study of harmony you will discover that it is the chord formed on the Tonic which determines the key of a piece of music. The character given to the melody and harmony by virtue of their relation to the Tonic is called **Tonality.**[1]

A melody is constructed from the following factors :

(1) Notes ascending or descending the Diatonic Scale (Major or Minor) of the key in which it is written.

(2) Notes ascending or descending the Chromatic Scale.

(3) Repeated or prolonged notes.

(4) Notes based on harmony (*i.e.* chords broken, or taken in **arpeggio**).

------

[1] In modern music the boundaries of tonality have been enlarged to include **polytonality** (the simultaneous use of different tonalities) and **atonality** (in which there is no relation to a central Key-note) ; neither comes within the scope of this book

Since a melody which proceeded entirely by step up and down the scale, or by leap to the different notes of a chord, or by the repetition or prolongation of the same note, would quickly become monotonous, at least two of the above factors are usually combined.

EXAMPLE 28

Admiral Benbow. 18TH CENTURY TUNE

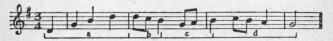

In Example 28, *a* is based on the common chord formed on the Tonic, and *b*, *c*, and *d* on the Diatonic Major Scale.

Though it may appear something of a paradox to suggest harmony as an element of melody, yet it is almost impossible to compose a good melody without thinking (perhaps unconsciously) of the harmonic structure. Even folk tunes, which were written with no idea of accompaniment, almost invariably suggest some kind of harmony. It must not be thought, however, that the harmonic structure of a melody is in any way inevitable ; there are always various ways of harmonizing a melody, and often its character may be completely changed by different harmony.

We have seen that the Diatonic Scale is not composed of equal intervals. Thus, a Major Scale has semitones between the 3rd and 4th, and 7th and 8th degrees. If you will examine a few simple melodies you will find that there is a closer affinity between those notes of the scale which are a semitone apart than between those which are a tone apart. Thus, in the scale of C Major, B is attracted to C rather than A, and E to F rather than D, so that when either of these notes moves by step it tends to rise a semitone rather than fall a tone. Similarly C tends to fall to B, and F to E. This attraction is exemplified in the first six bars of *God Save the Queen*.

EXAMPLE 29

Any one of these notes *may*, of course, move in the opposite direction, especially if it forms part of a scale passage, as in the second bar of Example 29. But it is useful to observe the general tendency. In the Harmonic Minor Scale semitones fall between the 2nd and 3rd, 5th and 6th, and 7th and 8th degrees, so that these notes tend to move towards one another. By far the strongest tendency, in both Major and Minor Scales, is for the Leading Note to rise to the Tonic, or " home " note.

Much akin is the tendency of the tonality to pull back a chromatic note (*i.e.* a note which does not belong to the key) to the nearest diatonic note of the key.

EXAMPLE 30
Minuet in G. BEETHOVEN

You will see that each time the melody strays from the key it is at once attracted back.

Cadences

In reading a verse such as the following[1]

" I know a thing that's most uncommon ;
    (Envy, be silent and attend !)
I know a reasonable woman,
    Handsome and witty, yet a friend."

---

[1] *On a certain Lady at Court.* (Alexander Pope.)

it is natural to make a slight pause at the end of each line, and perhaps to take a fresh breath before going on. A melody also has points of repose which divide it into units, or phrases. These points of repose are known as **Cadences,** and serve very much the same purpose as punctuation marks in literature. A cadence is literally a " fall," and just as in speech it is natural for the voice to fall at the end of a sentence, so in music there is a falling off in flow and movement (but not necessarily a fall in pitch) at a cadence.

EXAMPLE 31

All Through the Night.   WELSH MELODY

Play Example 31, and you will feel this falling off in bars 3 and 4, 7 and 8, and 15 and 16. The cadence used at these points is called a **Full Close** because the melody returns to the Tonic. The Full Close has a conclusive effect which may be compared with that of the full stop.

But punctuation is not confined to the full stop. Smith minor might begin an essay thus :

" This essay is about Tim. Tim is my dog. His coat is black. It is soft. He has white paws."

Such writing is felt to be irritating because it lacks continuity. No sooner do we get going than we are pulled up with a jerk. A more accomplished essayist might write :

" This essay is about my dog Tim.   He has a soft black coat, and white paws."

Here the commas though slowing up the flow of words do not bring it to a standstill.

The essence of a good melody being an easy and natural flow, the composer often introduces, during the course of a melody, cadences which produce the effect of temporary repose, without giving the impression that the melody has come to an end.   Such cadences, which correspond to the comma or semi-colon, are known as **Half Closes.**   A melodic Full Close normally consists of the Tonic preceded by a note of the common chord formed on the Dominant (*i.e.* the Supertonic, the Dominant, or the Leading Note).   A Half Close consists of the exact opposite, that is, the Tonic followed by a note of the Dominant Chord.

Melodic Shape

The two principal constituents of melody are Shape and Rhythm.

The shape of a melody may be simply defined as the upward and downward movement of the notes.   It is of little value to consider shape by itself, for melody is dependent upon rhythm for most of its character.   In Example 32 the time and rhythm of a well-known melody have been changed, but the melodic shape exactly preserved.   Play it, and you will find that the original melody[1] has been so altered in character as to be scarcely recognizable in its new form.

EXAMPLE 32

---

[1] The first six bars of *God Save the Queen.*

Nevertheless, the need for variety of shape must not be overlooked. Though it would be going altogether too far to say that every melody which has a graceful up and down movement is a good melody, melodies which lack variety of shape will often be found to be unsatisfactory. A melody should never wander aimlessly ; it should always be " going somewhere." (It has been said of ultra-modern melody that nobody but the composer knows, or cares, where it is going.)

A good melody should have a point of climax, some outstanding feature which forms the culmination of the whole melody. At this point there is frequently (but not invariably) a rise in pitch. The reason is that animation, and intensity of feeling, is increased when pitch is raised, and decreased when it is lowered. The climax of *God Save the Queen* is a good example ; it occurs in the last bar but one.

EXAMPLE 33

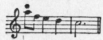

Notice that the climatic note (marked with an asterisk) is the highest of the melody, and is used for the first time ; had it been heard before the effect of the climax would have been considerably lessened.

Though, as might be expected, the point of climax often occurs towards the end of a melody, this is by no means the rule. In Example 31, for instance, the climatic note (E) comes in bar 10—little more than half-way through the melody.[1] Since the point of climax arises naturally from the curve and flow of the melody, its position cannot be predetermined with any

---

[1] In this melody also the effect of the climax is not weakened by the earlier use of the climatic note.

accuracy ; it is of little use the composer saying to himself " I will write a melody in which the climatic point occurs in the second beat of bar twelve." But if when a melody is constructed he feels that it lacks climax, or that the climatic point comes too early or too late, he may remedy this by the revision of the melodic shape or rhythm, or both. It is surprising how a small and seemingly unimportant alteration will often improve a melody almost beyond recognition.

Rhythm

Rhythm is difficult to define accurately. It is a combination of time, accent, and other elements, and is often confused with one or other of these.

In discussing rhythm it is useful to draw an analogy between poetry and music. Both, to be intelligible, must be grouped into more or less regular periods, and punctuated. Words are punctuated by means of stops ; music by means of cadences.

Each line of poetry, and each phrase[1] of music, has normally a certain number of regularly recurring strong and weak beats, which divide it into rhythmic units. In music these units are called bars.

In poetry strong and weak beats may be shown by placing the sign — over a strong beat, and ‿ over a weak one, thus :

" Ŏn Rīchmŏnd Hīll thĕre līves ă lāss."

No good actor would recite this line in a sing-song voice, as if he were scanning it ; but he would, nevertheless, make the rhythm underlie his words. In the same way, accent may be looked upon as underlying musical rhythm. The accentuation, or metre, of this line may be reproduced in music thus :

---

[1] " Phrase " is defined in a later chapter.

EXAMPLE 34

$$\frac{2}{4} \; \text{♩ | ♫ ♩ | ♫ ♩ | ♫ ♩ | ♩ ‖}$$

Since the accent (strong beat) occurs on alternate beats, the music is said to be in duple time.

Now consider this line :

" There's not in this wide world a valley so sweet."

The metre may be reproduced in music thus :

EXAMPLE 35

$$\frac{3}{4} \; \text{♩ | ♫ ♫ | ♫ ♫ | ♫ ♫ | ♩ ‖}$$

Here the accent occurs once in every three beats, and the music is said to be in triple time.

Musical accentuation is always divisible into groups of two or three beats—*i.e.* duple or triple time. Quadruple time ($\frac{4}{4}$, $\frac{4}{8}$, $\frac{12}{8}$, etc.) is really two bars of duple time compressed into one.

EXAMPLE 36

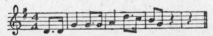

Example 36 could be written in $\frac{2}{4}$ time by dividing each bar into two equal parts, as shown by the dotted lines. In quadruple time, therefore, a strong accent occurs on the first of every two beats. In actual performance the accent on the third beat (sometimes called the secondary accent) is rather less marked than that on the first (primary accent).

Within each bar of a musical phrase the beat is usually divided into smaller combinations of notes—groups of half-beat notes, quarter-beat notes, and so on. By this means an infinite variety of rhythm is possible.

A phrase may begin and end on any beat, or portion of a beat.[1] Thus Example 36 begins on a non-accented beat (divided into a three-quarter-beat note and a quarter-beat note), and ends on an accented beat (divided into two half-beat notes).

When a phrase begins on an unaccented beat (or portion of a beat) the final bar is usually reduced by the number of beats which preceded the first accented beat of the phrase. A portion of the final bar is, in fact, borrowed to form the incomplete preliminary bar. Thus each of the sections into which Example 28 is divided begins on the third beat of the bar, and ends on the second beat. The last bar of the section is therefore reduced by the beat which preceded the first accented beat. By this means the end of the first section and the beginning of the second are dovetailed.[2]

In addition to the difference in strength between the beats of a bar, it will generally be found that bars themselves vary in weight, usually grouping themselves into alternately weak and strong bars.

EXAMPLE 37

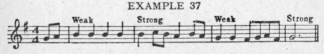

Strongly and weakly accented bars may usually be found by counting back from the bar which contains the final cadence. The cadence chord (*i.e.* the final chord of a cadence) almost invariably occurs on a strong accent, so that the bar before it will be weak, the bar before that strong, and so on.

---

[1] The note, or group of notes, occurring before the first accent is called the **anacrusis.**

[2] It is customary to omit from the last bar of a piece the beats which preceded the first accented beat; the last bar of Example 37, for instance, contains only three beats.

Music is sometimes inaccurately barred. Thus pieces may be found in $\frac{12}{8}$ time which should have been written in $\frac{6}{8}$ time. In waltzes, and other pieces in quick $\frac{3}{4}$ or $\frac{3}{8}$ time, every alternate bar usually receives so much greater stress than the previous one that the music is felt to be virtually in $\frac{6}{4}$ or $\frac{6}{8}$ time.

EXAMPLE 38

Treasure Waltz. JOHANN STRAUSS

Example 38 would be more accurately barred if two bars were thrown into one, thus :

EXAMPLE 39

Similarly, marches written in $\frac{2}{4}$ or $\frac{6}{8}$ time are often virtually in $\frac{4}{4}$ or $\frac{12}{8}$ time.

You see, then, that the bar-line is a convenient but arbitrary division, and that the only true measurement of rhythm is accent.

Syncopation

If the normal accent or beat is temporarily displaced, **Syncopation** is produced.

EXAMPLE 40

" *Carnaval.*" SCHUMANN, Op. 9

 *etc*

In Example 40 syncopation is effected (*a*) by placing an accented note on an unaccented beat (bars one and three), and (*b*) by tying a note on an unaccented beat to one on an accented beat (bars two and four). The altered accent is frequently marked with a stress (>), as in this example. Syncopation may occur in one part only, the accentuation of the other parts being normal, or the entire harmony may move in the same rhythm.

Though syncopation is a characteristic feature of modern dance music it is no new invention ; Bach and Handel both knew how to use it with good effect. Syncopation is " only a device for giving a little shake to the time."[1] Introduced in the right place at the right moment it may add a dash of spice to the rhythm ; used to excess it quickly becomes monotonous.

The Emotional Effect of Rhythm

The effect of long notes played at a slow pace is completely different from that of short notes played at a quick pace. The former gives an impression of dignity or calm ; the latter of restlessness or excitement. Thus the effect of working up to a climax may be obtained by successively shortening the length of the notes (*i.e.* using more and more notes in a bar). A similar effect may be obtained by increasing the pace of the music. The excitement is further intensified if there is also a gradual *crescendo* and a gradual rise in pitch. But even where the pace remains constant an almost unlimited

---

[1] W. R. Anderson in *The Musical Companion* (Gollancz).

variation of rhythmic effect is possible. Example 41
shows a few rhythmical arrangements of the first five
notes of the major scale, in $\frac{2}{4}$ time.

EXAMPLE 41

(a) The notes are presented in a straight-forward
form.

(b) The rhythm is enlivened by the introduction of
dotted notes.

(c) The notes are separated by rests, and would be
performed **staccato** (*i.e.* detached from one another).

(d) The rest introduced on an accented beat has a
marked effect on the rhythm.

(e) A rest is introduced on an unaccented beat ; the
effect is less marked than at (d).

(f) With the introduction of the triplet this example
is virtually in $\frac{6}{8}$ time ; there is consequently a marked
alteration of rhythm.

(g) The accent is shifted, the first two notes falling
on a weak beat instead of a strong one.

(h) The normal accent is displaced, producing
syncopation.

Rules of Melodic Progression

For the time being you should design your melodies
for voices, not instruments, for this will help you to
develop a smooth, vocal style of writing. Voices are
classified in four main groups : Soprano, Alto (or Contralto), Tenor, and Bass. The approximate compass of

each group, which should not normally be exceeded, is as follows :

EXAMPLE 42

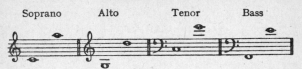

Soprano   Alto   Tenor   Bass

You should use the highest and lowest notes of each voice sparingly, keeping as a rule to the middle part of the compass.

The rules which follow should be rigidly observed in your early attempts at melodic construction. for like all rules they must be thoroughly learned before they can safely be broken.

(1) As far as possible move either by step (*i.e.* from one degree of the scale to the degree above or below it), or by leap of a consonant interval.

(2) As a general rule avoid the leap of a major seventh, all leaps beyond an octave and all augmented intervals. These leaps are unvocal, but it should be borne in mind that many intervals which are difficult for the voice are easy for an instrument, and may be freely used in instrumental writing.

(3) If a melody moves by a diminished interval let it return to a note *within* that interval.

EXAMPLE 3

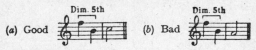

(*a*) Good   Dim. 5th   (*b*) Bad   Dim. 5th

(4) When the melody leaps a 6th or an octave, let the note preceding and following the leap be *within it.*

EXAMPLE 44

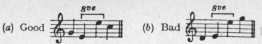

(a) Good   (b) Bad

(5) As a general rule let the Leading Note rise to the Octave,[1] unless it is in the middle of a descending scale passage.

EXAMPLE 45

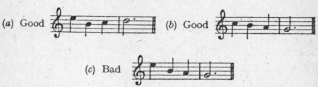

(a) Good   (b) Good

(c) Bad

(6) A succession of large leaps is usually ugly.

You should now be in a position to attempt the construction of short vocal melodies upon a given rhythmic scheme. Given this rhythm, for example,

EXAMPLE 46

you might construct this melody in C Major,

EXAMPLE 47

or this one in G Minor.

EXAMPLE 48

---

[1] In Chapter VII you will learn that the Leading Note may fall when a chord changes position.

Exercises

1. Write several different vocal melodies upon each of the rhythms given, in various major and minor keys. In (a) and (b) start with the Tonic; in (c) and (d) with the Dominant. End each melody with a Full Close, and use a Half Close at points marked with a square bracket.

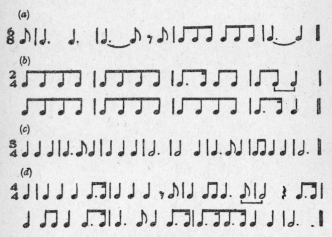

2. Construct twelve different rhythmical arrangements of each of the following, in the manner of Example 41.

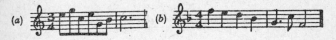

3. Analyse as many melodies as possible under the following headings (national songs and folk melodies are particularly useful):

(a) Factors from which the melody is constructed

(Diatonic or Chromatic scale passages, repeated or prolonged notes, and notes based on chords).

(*b*) Shape (variety of curve ; and point of climax, if any).

(*c*) Cadences (Full or Half Closes).

(*d*) Rhythm (the effect of dotted notes, rests, triplets, syncopation, etc.).

CHAPTER IV

TRIADS

If we regard any note of the scale as a bass note, or **root**, and place above it two other notes, one a third and the other a fifth from the root, we form the simplest complete chord in music—the **Triad** (*i.e.* the union of three different notes).

If we place the third and the fifth notes of the Major Scale above the Tonic, we form a Major Triad.

EXAMPLE 49

KEY OF C MAJOR

We may form Triads on each degree of the Major or Minor Scale, using only the notes of the scale itself.

EXAMPLE 50

KEY OF C MAJOR

You will see from Example 50 that of the Triads formed on the seven degrees of the Major Scale, three are Major, three Minor, and one Diminished. Careful examination will show the following differences between the three kinds of Triads.

(1) A Major Triad is formed by placing above a root (or bass note) two notes, a **major** third and a **perfect** fifth from the root.

(2) A Minor Triad is formed by placing above a root two notes, a **minor** third and a **perfect** fifth from the root.

(3) A Diminished Triad is formed by placing above a root two notes, a **minor** third and a **diminished** fifth from the root.

For convenience each Triad is distinguished by a Roman numeral which shows the degree of the scale on which it is formed. Thus I means a Triad formed on the Tonic, II one formed on the Supertonic, and so on.

The principal Triads in any major or minor key are those formed on the Tonic, Subdominant, and Dominant degrees of the scale (indicated by the Roman numerals I, IV, V). These are known as the **Primary Triads,**[1] and form, as it were, the backbone of the key. Those Triads which are formed on other degrees of the scale are known as the **Secondary Triads.**

It is of the utmost importance that you should be able to distinguish the different characteristics of the three kinds of Triads. Play each separately, listening carefully to the effect. Notice that the Major and Minor Triads sound complete in themselves ; this is because they are made up of consonant intervals—a major or minor third, and a perfect fifth. The difference between a Major and Minor Triad will at once be felt if one is followed by the other, thus :

EXAMPLE 51

The effect of the Major Triad is cheerful ; that of the

---

[1] A Triad of which the fifth is perfect is known as a Common Chord.

Minor Triad sad. When we play Example 51, we feel as if we are passing from the sunshine into the gloom.

The Diminished Triad, being formed from a consonant interval (a minor third) and a dissonant interval (a diminished fifth) is dissonant (*i.e.* it sounds incomplete until it is resolved upon a consonant chord, as in Example 52).

EXAMPLE 52

Each kind of Triad requires different treatment, and for the present we shall concern ourselves only with the Primary Triads of the major key, each of which is a Major Triad.

A Triad, as we have seen, consists of three different sounds, and no chord may be considered complete which has fewer than three sounds. If a fourth sound is added to a Triad it is evident that one of the three sounds must be doubled in another octave ; but the chord, nevertheless, remains a Triad, since it contains only three *different* notes. Similarly, a chord of five or six notes may be formed by doubling two or three notes of the Triad.

The notes of a Triad (whether there are three, four, or more) admit of considerable variety of arrangement, for although the root always remains the same, the highest note of the Triad may be one of three notes.

EXAMPLE 53

Example 53 shows six of the many different ways in which it is possible to arrange the Major Triad which has C as its root. Let us consider each in turn :

(*a*) is the normal arrangement of a three-note Triad ; E (the middle note) is a major third, and G (the top note) a perfect fifth, above the root. Such a Triad is said to be in **close** position, because the notes lie as close together as possible.

(*b*) is said to be in **open** position, because the notes are spaced out at wider intervals. E now becomes the top note, but is still a major third from the root (it is actually a major tenth away, but a tenth, as we have seen, is really a compound third). G becomes the middle note, still a perfect fifth from the root.

(*c*) is not a complete Triad, since the fifth from the root is missing. But it is sometimes used in this form, the ear accepting it as a Triad by imagining the missing G.

(*d*) is a four-note Triad in close position. Notice that the top note merely doubles the root at the octave.

(*e*) and (*f*) are open positions of a four-note Triad. Again the root is doubled.

Exercises

1. Play and write Major, Minor, and Diminished Triads in various keys, carefully noting the difference in effect between them. Continue this exercise until you are able to distinguish between the three kinds of Triads (*a*) by ear alone, at the piano, and (*b*) by eye (and calculation) alone, away from the piano.

2. Write Major Triads on each of the roots given below, arranging each Triad in at least six different ways. Use close and open positions, and three- and four-part harmony. G, F, E, D, B flat, A, E flat, E, A flat.

CHAPTER V

THE ADDITION OF A BASS TO A MELODY

Four-part writing is the foundation of modern harmony, and although few compositions (with the exception of hymn tunes) remain in four-part harmony throughout, practice in four-part writing is the surest method by which the principles of harmony may be grasped.

For the time being we shall regard four-part harmony as being designed for four voices ; soprano, alto, tenor, and bass. The highest part (which we may call the melody) will be taken by the soprano voice, the lowest part (which we may call the bass) by the bass voice, and the two inner parts by the alto and tenor voices.

In writing harmony for three, four, or more voices, we have to consider the relation not only between the different chords, but also the different voice parts. This means that (a) the progression between chord and chord must be correct, and (b) the voice parts, while each observing the laws of melodic progression, must blend satisfactorily with one another. As it is easier to do one thing at a time than three or four, the melody should be constructed first, the bass part next, and finally the inner parts. (It is sometimes a useful exercise, however, to add a melody to a bass part.)

Let us first consider the addition of a bass part to a simple melody. For the present we are concerned only with the three Primary Triads, I, IV, and V. Every note of the major scale may be harmonized with one or other of these Triads.

The bass notes in Example 54 are, of course, the roots of three Primary Triads. The melody and bass parts together form the skeleton from which four-part harmony may be constructed. The effect of the two

EXAMPLE 54

I   V   I   IV I   IV V   I

parts is necessarily bare, because one note (or two notes when the soprano voice doubles the root) of the Triad is missing in each chord. It is only when a third part is added that the harmony becomes complete and satisfying.

In adding a bass part to a melody the choice of notes is at present limited to three—the roots of the Primary Triads. In the key of C these notes are C, F, and G ; in the key of G they are G, C, and D ; and so on. Your immediate concern is not so much the construction of a melodious bass part (this is scarcely possible with so limited a selection of notes) as of a part which, in addition to conforming to the rules of melodic progression, obeys the following rules :

(1) The bass must not move in consecutive fifths with the melody.

EXAMPLE 55

Bad

(2) The bass must not move in consecutive octaves with the melody.

EXAMPLE 56

Bad

(3) The bass must not move in consecutive unisons with the melody.

EXAMPLE 57

Bad

Consecutive fifths, octaves, and unisons are only objectionable if they are *moving* ; the repetition of the same fifth, octave, or unison is always allowed. Experienced composers frequently use progressions in which these consecutives appear, but the beginner must learn to observe the rules before he can safely break them.

EXAMPLE 58

Example 58 is free from forbidden consecutives. But had F (IV) been used as the third bass note consecutive fifths would have been formed.

EXAMPLE 59

Bad

I   V   IV   I

Similarly, had G (the root of V) been used as the fifth bass note, consecutive octaves would have resulted.

EXAMPLE 60

Bad

I   V   I   V

The ugly effect of these examples will probably be apparent if they are played, but would be much more so if the inner parts were added.

Exercises

1. Add bass parts to the following melodies, using only the roots of the Primary Triads. Play over the completed exercises, listening carefully to the movement of the two parts, and watching for forbidden consecutives. (*N.B.*—The Tonic Triad should be used when possible. The melody note C, for instance, forms part of the Triads I and IV in the key of C ; I should be chosen in preference to IV). Two notes whose letter names are adjacent (*e.g.* F, G in the key of C) should be written a 2nd apart, and not a 7th. Each melody should begin with the Tonic root, and end with a Full Close (the Dominant root followed by the Tonic Root).

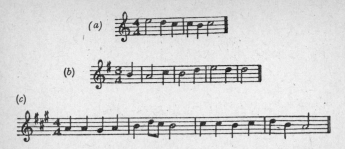

2. Add melodies to the following basses, playing the two parts over and checking for consecutives as before. Make the melodies as smooth and tuneful as possible, and do not use the same note twice in succession. (*N.B.*—The letter above the first note of each exercise shows the note on which the melody should begin. For the other notes you have three possible choices to each bass note. Thus you could add C, E, or G to the bass note C; F, A, or C to the bass note F; and so on.) Each melody should end with a Full Close (a note of the Dominant Triad followed by a note of the Tonic Triad).

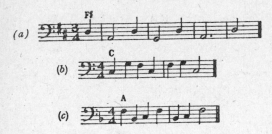

CHAPTER VI

FOUR-PART CHORDS

We must next consider the addition of two inner parts to existing soprano and bass parts, so as to form four-part harmony. These additional parts should be designed for alto and tenor voices. The soprano and alto parts may be written on the treble stave, and the tenor and bass parts on the bass stave, the tails of the soprano and tenor notes being turned up, and those of the alto and bass notes down (*see* Example 66).

Since there are only three different notes in a Triad— the root, the third from the root, and the fifth from the root—it is clear that one of these notes must be doubled in four-part harmony. In a Major Triad it is usually best to double the root in preference to the fifth, and the fifth in preference to the third.

As we saw in Chapter IV, there are several alternative arrangements of the Triad. Example 61 shows some of the forms in which the Tonic Triad in the key of C Major may appear.

EXAMPLE 61

The root (C) is doubled in all these chords except in the one marked (*a*), in which the fifth is doubled.

Sometimes the fifth of the chord may be left out, and the root placed in three voices.

EXAMPLE 62

The third of the chord should not be omitted since without it the Triad loses its character. To prove this play the perfect fifth C to G on the piano, and then add the major third, E. The fifth immediately becomes a Major Triad. Now play the fifth again, this time adding the minor third, E flat. The fifth now becomes a Minor Triad. You see, then, that it is the third which gives the Triad its character of Major or Minor.

In arranging chords for four voices it is important that the parts shall be properly spaced, or balanced. In order to secure good balance the gap between the soprano and alto, and alto and tenor parts, should not exceed an octave. The tenor and bass parts may, if necessary, be more than an octave apart. The spacing of the chords in Example 61 conforms to these principles, and should be carefully studied.

Similar, Contrary, and Oblique Motion

The way in which the different voices, or parts, of the harmony move together is called **Harmonic Progression.** In harmonic progression there are three different kinds of motion :

(1) Two or more parts may move in the same direction. This is called

Similar Motion

EXAMPLE 63

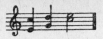

(2) Two parts may move in opposite directions. This is called

Contrary Motion

EXAMPLE 64

(3) A part may rise or fall while another remains stationary. This is called

Oblique Motion

EXAMPLE 65

When three or four parts move together, two or three kinds of motion are usually combined.

EXAMPLE 66

In Example 66 the first two notes of the soprano part move in contrary motion with the bass, in similar motion with the tenor, and in oblique motion with the

alto ; the last two notes of the soprano part move in similar motion with the alto and bass, and in contrary motion with the tenor.

Exercises

1. Add alto and tenor parts to the following so as to form Primary Triads.

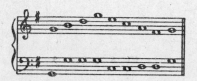

2. Arrange, in properly spaced four-part harmony, each of the Primary Triads (I, IV, V) in the following Major keys ; D, F, B flat, A, E flat, E, A flat.

3. Take any simple hymn tune in four parts, and determine the motion (similar, contrary, or oblique) of the soprano part in relation to the other parts. Do the same with the alto, tenor, and bass parts.

CHAPTER VII

HARMONIC PROGRESSION

Rules of Harmonic Progression

Having seen how separate chords may be built up, you must now learn to connect them together. There are certain definite rules of harmonic progression, and these you should memorize, first making quite sure that you understand their correct application.

(1) Make each part flow as smoothly as possible by avoiding unnecessary movement. When two consecutive chords have a note in common, it should generally be kept in the same part.

EXAMPLE 67

In Example 67 the note C appears in the tenor part of both chords, and so acts as a connecting link.

(2) As far as possible let each moving part go to the nearest note of the next chord.

EXAMPLE 68

(a) Good   (b) Clumsy

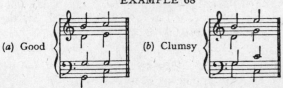

In Example 68 (*a*) is good because each part (except the tenor, which remains stationary) moves to the next nearest note ; (*b*) is clumsy because the three upper parts make awkward leaps.

(3) Let each part observe the rules of melodic progression (*see* Chapter III). One modification should be noted, however. The leading note may fall (in any part) if the same chord changes from one position to another.

EXAMPLE 69

(4) Avoid overlapping of parts.

EXAMPLE 70

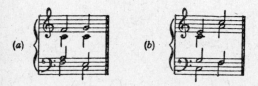

Example 70 shows two specimens of overlapping. In (*a*) the second note of the tenor part falls below the first note of the bass ; and in (*b*) the second note of the alto part rises above the first note of the soprano.

There is one exception to this rule. When a chord moves to a higher position of the same chord (as in Example 71) overlapping of parts is permissible.

EXAMPLE 71

(5) Avoid consecutive unisons, fifths, and octaves (*see* Chapter V) between the same pair of parts.

(6) Do not let the highest and lowest parts approach an octave or a fifth by *similar* motion, except where the highest part moves by step.

EXAMPLE 72

(*a*) Good

(*b*) Bad   (*c*) Good

Connexion of Chords

The chords which follow one another most naturally are those which have one or more notes in common to connect them together.

Of the primary triads I and IV, and I and V, have

a note in common. Let us first consider the connexion between I and V.

EXAMPLE 73

Play Example 73 several times, listening carefully to the effect of the last two chords. The middle chord (V) has a feeling of incompleteness, of the expectation of some other chord to follow; this is largely due to the presence of the Leading Note of the scale, with its strong upward tendency. The last chord (I) has a feeling of completeness and final repose.

The Perfect Cadence

Because of its conclusive effect, the chord progression of Dominant to Tonic is nearly always used at the end of a composition. (To prove this look through any book of hymn tunes.) This progression is called a **Perfect Cadence,** or **Full Close.** (A melody does not wander on continuously, but is made up of sentences and phrases, each of which has a more or less definite ending. This ending is usually harmonized by means of a succession of two chords known as a **Cadence.** There are four different kinds of cadences in general use.)

The effect of the Perfect Cadence is greatly strengthened if the two chords which form it are preceded by a chord other than the Tonic Triad. The Subdominant Triad (IV) forms an excellent approach.

EXAMPLE 74

The Imperfect Cadence

If the Dominant Triad is preceded by some other chord (for the time being either I or IV) another kind of cadence is formed.

EXAMPLE 75

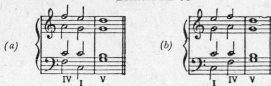

Example 75 shows the Dominant Triad preceded by (*a*) the Tonic Triad, and (*b*) the Subdominant Triad. Each of these progressions produces the effect of temporary rest, much less final than that of the Perfect Cadence, and is called an **Imperfect Cadence,** or **Half Close.** Play Example 75 listening carefully to the effect. Note that when the final chord (V) is preceded by I as in (*a*), IV forms a good approach ; and that when it is preceded by IV as in (*b*), I forms a good approach. The Imperfect Cadence is frequently used to end any phrase other than the last one of a piece.

The Plagal Cadence

Yet another kind of cadence is formed when the Subdominant Triad is followed by the Tonic Triad.

EXAMPLE 76

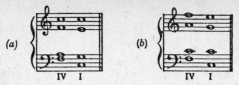

Play Example 76, which shows two positions of this cadence, and you will find that this is the progression which is almost invariably used to harmonize the word " Amen " at the end of a hymn tune. It is called a **Plagal Cadence.** The effect of the Plagal Cadence is even more conclusive than that of the Perfect Cadence, and for this reason it is rarely used except at the end of a piece. Its purpose is usually to extend a Perfect Cadence and strengthen its effect.

EXAMPLE 77

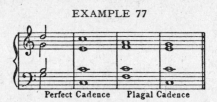

Perfect Cadence   Plagal Cadence

Notice that the Perfect Cadence in Example 77 has the fifth of the Tonic Triad omitted, in order to allow the Leading Note to rise correctly to the Tonic.

The Progression IV to V, and V to IV

The Triads on the Subdominant and Dominant have no note in common, and when one of these chords is followed by the other care must be taken to avoid consecutive fifths and octaves.

When IV is followed by V, at least two of the upper parts should move in contrary motion with the bass (as in Example 74, page 69).

EXAMPLE 78

EXAMPLE 78

Bad

IV V I

In Example 78 this rule is disregarded, with the result that consecutive octaves occur between the alto and bass parts, and consecutive fifths between the tenor and bass parts.

Similarly, when V is followed by IV at least two of the upper parts should move in contrary motion with the bass. It is usually best to let the soprano part move from the fifth of V to the root of IV, as in Example 79.

EXAMPLE 79

Good

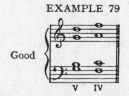

V IV

In harmonizing a given melody or bass part, the bass (or melody) should first be added, and the alto and tenor parts then filled in. Try to make the highest and lowest parts move in contrary motion as far as possible.

Accent

We must next consider how accent affects the choice of chords. We have seen that the end of a musical phrase is marked by a cadence, the first chord of which generally occurs on a weak accent, and the second (the cadence chord) on a strong accent.[1] The recommendations which follow will help you to construct a progression of chords which leads satisfactorily to the cadence.

(1) Do not use the same chord from a weak to a strong accent, except at the start of a piece.

EXAMPLE 80

(2) If the first chord of a piece falls on a strong beat it is usually best to start with the Tonic Chord. If the first chord occurs on a weak beat it is usually best to start with either the Tonic or the Dominant Chord. This ensures a proper definition of the Tonic key.

EXAMPLE 81

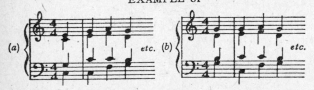

Example 81 shows the application of this rule. In both examples the first chord occurs on a weak beat : (a) starts with the Tonic Chord, and proceeds to another position of the same chord ; (b) starts with the Dominant Chord, and proceeds to the Tonic Chord.

---

[1] The cadence chord does sometimes fall on a weak accent ; the cadence chord of the Tango usually ends on the second beat of the bar, and that of the Polonaise on the third beat.

(3) When writing in triple time do not use the same chord from one weak accent to another, unless it is also used on the preceding strong accent. You may, however, use the same chord from a strong to a weak accent.

EXAMPLE 82

(a) Bad

(b) Good

In Example 82 (a) is bad because the same chord is used from one weak accent to another; (b) is good because the same chord is used from a strong accent to the weak accent which succeeds it.

Exercises

1. (i) Figure each chord (I, IV, or V).
   (ii) Name each cadence (there are two cadences in *d*).
   (iii) Add alto and tenor parts.

2. Play on the piano the examples given in this chapter of Perfect, Imperfect (I, V and IV, V), and Plagal Cadences. Then transpose each example into the following keys: G, F, B flat, D, E flat, A, A flat, E. You may find it easier to play the three upper parts with the right hand and the bass part with the left.

3. Without reference to the examples in this chapter play on the piano Perfect, Imperfect, and Plagal Cadences in the keys named above.

4. Add bar-lines to the following, paying particular attention to correct accentuation. Then add alto and tenor parts.

5. Add alto, tenor, and bass parts to the following (add the bass part first).

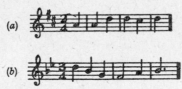

6. Add parts for alto, tenor, and bass to the three melodies in Exercise I, Chapter V. Add the bass part first.

7. Add parts for soprano, alto, and tenor to the three basses in Exercise 2, Chapter V. Add the soprano part first.

CHAPTER VIII

PHRASE BUILDING

In Chapter III we saw that both poetry and music have regularly recurring beats and accents. Let us now take the analogy a step further.

Consider these lines :

" Way down upon de Swanee ribber,
    Far, far away,
  Dere's where my heart is turning ebber,
    Dere's where de old folks stay."

This verse expresses a complete idea, and in order to make it intelligible it is divided into lines and phrases, and punctuated. In the same way a complete musical idea is made up of smaller periods. A melody may generally be split up into sections (of two or more notes), phrases (of two or more sections), and sentences (of two or more phrases).

To make this clear let us analyse a simple melodic idea.

EXAMPLE 83

The Old Folks at Home. STEPHEN FOSTER

Example 83 constitutes, in its entirety, a sentence expressing a complete musical idea, and ending, as it were, with a full stop. This sentence may be divided into two equal phrases, and the phrases subdivided into two equal sections.

Compare the verse of *The Old Folks at Home* with the music, and you will find that each exhibits the same kind of symmetry. Thus the first line of the verse rhymes with the third, and the second line with the fourth ; similarly the first section of the music is exactly imitated by the third, and the second section nearly imitated by the fourth. Symmetry therefore exists between the two phrases, and between the sections which make up each phrase.

Sometimes one or both sections of a phrase may be divided into smaller groups of notes called " figures."

EXAMPLE 84

The Bay of Biscay. J. DAVY

Example 84 may be divided into two half-sections (figures) and one whole section ; the phrase as a whole is symmetrical, one half balancing the other. It is clear, therefore, that a phrase may exhibit symmetry whether its divisions are similar or dissimilar in length.

Between the phrase divisions there may be either similarity or diversity of rhythm and melody. Thus in Example 85 the second bar is an exact imitation of the first, whereas the fourth bar is an imitation by **inversion** (*i.e.* the rhythm is the same, but the interval of the melody is inverted).

EXAMPLE 85

Ballet Music (Rosamunde). SCHUBERT

The second figure in Example 84 (*The Bay of Biscay*)
is a reproduction of the previous figure at a higher pitch.[1]
The first four notes of the second section are also founded
on this melodic figure (in a different rhythm).

Between the first and second, and third and fourth,
sections of Example 83 (*The Old Folks at Home*) there is
rhythmic and melodic diversity.

Very often a figure or section which is repeated is
presented in a modified form to avoid the monotony of
an exact repetition.

EXAMPLE 86

The Bailiff's Daughter. TRADITIONAL

Thus, in Example 86 (*b*) is a modified version of (*a*).
Such a modification should proceed from longer notes to
shorter notes, not *vice versa ;* if (*b*) were followed by (*a*)
for instance, the interest would be decreased instead of
increased.

It is not necessary—and often undesirable—that all
the divisions of a phrase or sentence should be of equal
length.   A beginner, asked to add a responsive section
to the following :

---

[1] This comparative repetition is called a **Sequence**.

EXAMPLE 87

might continue thus :

EXAMPLE 88

Compare this with the answering section which Mendelssohn wrote :

EXAMPLE 89

How much more artistic than the previous example, with its slavish imitation of the rhythmic pattern ! Here we have two figures, each a bar in length, balanced by a two-bar section which runs without a break. Such a division is quite often met with—*see* Examples 84 and 85 in this chapter. More rarely the first section is continuous, and the second divisible into figures ; Example 153 on page 133 is subdivided in this way.

Example 87 is a good illustration of how a phrase may be built up from a single idea consisting of a few notes. The idea contained in the first figure is repeated (a fourth higher) in the second figure, and is also made use of (in an inverted form) in the last part of the second section (Example 89).

Most popular melodies—waltzes, marches, dance tunes, and so on—are more or less symmetrical in structure, for in music intended for dancing or marching regularity is usually essential. Other forms of music are often less symmetrical; a sentence may consist of three phrases,[1] instead of two or four, and a phrase may be composed of unequal sections. These slight departures from absolute symmetry and regularity come as a relief to the ear, and prevent the musical structure from becoming stiff and " square-toed."

The phrase, which is the most convenient unit from which to measure other periods, consists, in its most usual form, of four bars of music.[2] We have seen, however, that music in quick $\frac{3}{4}$ or $\frac{3}{8}$, and $\frac{2}{4}$ or $\frac{6}{8}$ time is often incorrectly barred, two bars virtually counting as one.[3] For this reason most quick waltzes and marches are composed of eight-bar phrases, which are usually divisible into two four-bar sections.

We have seen that a phrase usually begins with the Tonic or Dominant Chord, and ends with a cadence. Cadences may be compared to the punctuation marks used in literature. The last phrase of a musical sentence usually ends with a Perfect or Plagal cadence, either of which gives the effect of complete repose, and corresponds to the full stop. The first phrase usually ends with an Imperfect or an Interrupted Cadence,[4] which gives the effect of pause without finality, and corresponds to the comma, semicolon, or question mark.

When, however, an intermediate phrase ends with a

---

[1] Since it is more difficult to think in groups of threes than in groups of twos, sentences of three phrases are decidedly rare. The most familiar example of a three-phrase sentence is the first part of *God Save the Queen*, which consists of three phrases of two bars each.

[2] Hymn tunes are often composed in two-bar phrases.

[3] *See* page 45.

[4] The use of the Interrupted Cadence is discussed in Chapter XIV.

Perfect Cadence, the effect of finality may often be avoided if the melody is given the third or fifth of the cadence chord, instead of the root. To test this play the first phrase (*i.e.* the first four bars) of *Nearer My God to Thee*—the well-known hymn tune by the Rev. J. B. Dykes—followed by the last phrase. You will find that although the two phrases are almost identical, the effect of the first phrase, in which the melody takes the third of the cadence chord, is much less conclusive than that of the last phrase, where the melody takes the root.

When a phrase can be divided into sections it is often better to avoid a cadence, except at the end of the final section.[1]

A single phrase, even though it ends with a Perfect Cadence, cannot form a complete sentence until it is joined by another phrase. As Professor Prout (1835–1909) aptly put it "one phrase by itself is as incomplete as half a pair of scissors."[2] Look again at Example 83 and you will see that the second phrase is an almost exact imitation of the first ; each phrase, in fact, is the complement of the other. In sentences which are made up of two symmetrical phrases, the initial phrase is almost invariably succeeded by a complementary, or " responsive," phrase.

In regular two-phrase sentences symmetry may be obtained in three ways.

(1) The responsive phrase may be (*a*) an exact, or (*b*) an almost exact, repetition of the initial phrase.

Example of (*a*) :
The Last Rose of Summer[3] (1st 8 bars).

---

[1] This is only a general recommendation ; intermediate sections often end with an Imperfect, or even a Perfect, Cadence.

[2] *Musical Form* (Augener).

[3] All these examples, together with many other national melodies, may be found in *Songs of the British Islands*, edited by W. H. Hadow (Curwen).

Example of (*b*) :

The Old Folks at Home (*see* page 75).

In this tune the only difference between the two phrases is that the initial phrase ends on an Imperfect Cadence, and the responsive phrase on a Perfect Cadence.

(2) The responsive phrase may imitate the initial phrase in contrary motion (*i.e.* the melody of the one phrase may move largely in the opposite direction to that of the other, but in similar rhythm). This structure is comparatively rare.

Example :

Hearts of Oak (1st 8 bars).

(3) The melody and rhythm of the responsive phrase may be contrasted with that of the initial phrase.

Example :

Rule, Britannia (1st 10 bars).

The art of building musical sentences lies in the balancing of two opposing forces—Unity and Variety. Unity demands the welding together of the various divisions into a coherent and continuous idea ; Variety the avoidance of monotony by a degree of diversity and contrast. It is impossible to formulate definite rules for carrying out these conditions. The careful analysis of melodies on the lines suggested in this chapter will show how Unity in Variety may be achieved, but the precise means to be adopted in a particular case depend on the judgment and experience of the composer.

Your first attempts should be the composition of regular sentences consisting of two four-bar (or eight-bar) phrases. Each phrase should be constructed separately, the rhythm being first put down, and the melody then added. Let us build up a specimen sentence on these lines. First we jot down the rhythm of the opening phrase.

EXAMPLE 90

As this phrase is divisible into sections it will be artistic to make the responsive phrase continuous.

EXAMPLE 91

Finally, we build a melody on this rhythmic basis.

EXAMPLE 92

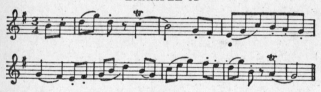

Notice that the first figure is repeated (in a modified form) in the last part of the second phrase. Observe also that we have not made the mistake (a common one with beginners) of continuing the second phrase with the same notes as those with which the first phrase started.

Exercises

1. Add responsive phrase to each of the following so as to form a complete musical sentence.

(a)

(b)

Allegro vivace

(c)

Gavotte

2. Clothe the following rhythms with melody, so as to form complete musical sentences.

(a)

Allegretto

(b)

Moderato

3. Construct original musical sentences consisting of two balanced phrases.

CHAPTER IX

MAJOR TRIADS (FIRST INVERSION)

So far we have regarded the root of a Triad as the bass note (*i.e.* the lowest note of the harmony). But since a Triad consists of three notes it is obvious that any one of these may be used as a bass note.

When the root of a Triad is in the bass, the Triad is said to be in **root position.** When either of the upper notes is in the bass, the Triad is said to be **inverted.** Two inversions are possible : (1) when the third from the root becomes the bass, and (2) when the fifth from the root becomes the bass.

In Example 93 the chords marked (*b*) are first

EXAMPLE 93

O Come all ye Faithful. ENGLISH (18th Century)

inversions, and the chord marked (*c*) is a second inversion.

You may wonder why these inversions are used, and

EXAMPLE 94

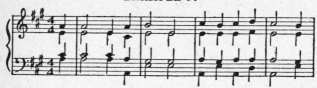

whether they really add anything to the music. A simple
experiment should convince you. First play Example 93,
listening carefully to the effect of the chord progression.
Follow this with Example 94, in which the same melody
is harmonized entirely with chords in root position. How
much clumsier and weaker it sounds when compared
with the previous example !

Each inversion needs separate consideration, and
for the moment we shall confine our attention to the
first inversion, in which the third of the chord appears
in the bass.

EXAMPLE 95

Example 95 shows the first inversion of the Tonic
Triad in the key of C Major. The letter *b* which is
placed beside the Roman numeral indicates a first
inversion. The use of these small letters, combined with
Roman numerals, is a convenient means of identifying
chords. In future *a* will be used to indicate the root
position of a chord, *b* the first inversion, and *c* the second
inversion. Thus I*a* means the root position of the
Tonic Triad, IV*b* the first inversion of the Subdominant
Triad, V*c* the second inversion of the Dominant Triad,
and so on.

EXAMPLE 96

Example 96 shows the three Primary Triads in the
key of C Major, in root position and first inversion. Play

each pair of chords separately, listening carefully so as to fix the effect of each chord in the mind. Better still, have the six chords played over to you (out of order) and say which are in root position and which in first inversion.

Persevere with these exercises until you are able to distinguish, by ear and by eye, between the root position of a chord and its first inversion.

You will see from Example 96 that by using the Primary Triads in root position and first inversion we now have a choice of six bass notes—one on every degree of the scale except the Supertonic. It is clear that by the judicious use of the first inversion we may avoid the ungainly and monotonous movement of the bass part which was inevitable when we had only three bass notes at our disposal.

EXAMPLE 97

Play Example 97 and you will readily appreciate the superiority of (a) and (c) over (b) and (d). When the melody moves from one note to another note of the same chord, as in (a), the use of a first inversion often prevents monotony. The first inversion in (c) produces a smoother bass part, and makes it unnecessary to repeat the root of the Dominant Triad in the next bar.

When a root position is followed by a first inversion of the *same* chord (or *vice versa*), the two chords should move from a strong accent to a weak one, not from a weak to a strong one. Compare Example 98 (a) (in which this recommendation is disregarded) with (b).

EXAMPLE 98

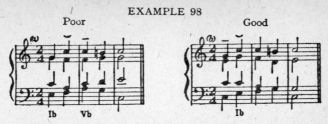

Poor   Good

Ib   Vb   Ib

In Example 97 (*c*) the tenor note is sustained throughout the two bars, instead of being repeated. When the same note occurs in the same part in successive chords it may either be repeated or sustained. Play Example 97 (*c*) as written, then play it again, repeating the tenor note with each chord. You will find that when the note is sustained it tends to bind the harmony together and give it a certain smoothness, but that when it is repeated the effect is rather more precise. Each method has its uses ; the choice of one or the other in a particular context is simply a matter of personal taste.

We have seen that the third of a Major Triad is the characteristic note of the chord, and should not normally be doubled in four-part harmony. This leaves us with the choice of two notes—the root and the fifth—either of which may be doubled.[1]

EXAMPLE 99

Good   Good   Poor

Ib   Ib   Ib

[1] The rules for doubling in the root position therefore apply to a first inversion.

Play Example 99 and you will notice the good effect of (*a*) in which the root is doubled and (*b*) in which the fifth is doubled, and the rather uncouth effect of (*c*) in which the third is doubled.

Of the six chords now at our disposal (*see* Example 96) two—IV and V—are consecutive first inversions. When these chords are used in succession care must be taken to avoid consecutives; if the soprano part moves in sixths with the bass the root and the fifth should be doubled alternately.

EXAMPLE 100

In Example 100 (*a*) the root is doubled in the first chord, and the fifth in the second; in (*b*) the root is doubled in both chords, producing consecutive fifths between the alto and tenor parts, and consecutive octaves between the soprano and tenor parts; in (*c*) the fifth is doubled in both chords, producing consecutive octaves between the alto and tenor parts.

EXAMPLE 101

The first inversion often provides a good approach to a cadence (*see* Example 101).

When either or both of the chords forming a cadence are not in root position, the cadence is said to be **inverted**. We have seen that the Full Close (*i.e.* the Perfect Cadence with both chords in root position) should generally be used at the end of a sentence ; but the Inverted Perfect Cadence (Va followed by Ib, or Vb followed by Ia) may be freely used for the middle cadences of a sentence. This type of cadence, which is shown in Example 102 (*a*) and (*b*), has a much less conclusive effect than that of the Full Close. Ia followed by Vb forms an Inverted Imperfect Cadence (*see* Example 102 (*c*)), which is often useful as an intermediate cadence.

EXAMPLE 102

By experimenting with chords in root position and first inversion you may discover which progressions are good, and which are not. It would serve no useful purpose to give a list of such progressions, since the effect of a particular progression depends to a great extent on the context. The rules and recommendations in this book will help you to write grammatical harmony, but you should never accept any rule without first testing the mental effect. Harmony is not necessarily good simply because it breaks no rules ; the ear, not the eye, must be the ultimate judge.

Exercises

(1) Add alto and tenor parts to the following:

(a)

(b)

(2) Improve the following passages by substituting a first inversion for a root position where appropriate. Do not alter the soprano part.

(a)   (b)

(3) Add parts for alto, tenor and bass.

* Repeat the previous chord.

(4) Add parts for soprano, alto, and tenor.

(a)   (b)

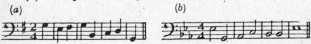

CHAPTER X

FIRST ATTEMPTS AT MUSICAL COMPOSITION

If you have mastered the preceding chapters you will now be in a position to attempt the composition of complete musical sentences. The resources at your immediate disposal are limited to the three Primary Triads in root position and first inversion ; but these simple chords are the backbone of harmony, and once you have really grasped their meaning you will be well on the way to the mastery of the remaining harmonic material.

Let us start by composing a complete musical sentence consisting of two four-bar phrases. In order to make the process quite clear we shall begin, as it were, with the skeleton, and gradually clothe it with flesh. First of all let us construct a rhythmic scheme.

EXAMPLE 103

This rhythm is perfectly regular, the second phrase being an exact imitation of the first. We know that at the end of each phrase there should be some sort of cadence. As the second phrase concludes the sentence we may end it with a Full Close. The end of the first phrase needs to be less conclusive, so an Imperfect or an Inverted Perfect Cadence will be best.

As the first note of the sentence falls on a weak beat we had better harmonize it with I or V, and proceed to I on the first strong accent. After consideration we decide to use an Imperfect Cadence at the end of the first phrase, a Full Close at the end of the last phrase, and the first inversion of the Tonic Triad, leading to the root position of the same chord, for the first two notes.

EXAMPLE 104

Ib Ia   Ia Va   Va Ia

We must next complete the bass, making it as smooth and melodious as possible. At this stage we shall find it helpful to think back from the cadences. We know that IV forms a good approach to either the Perfect or the Imperfect Cadence. In the first cadence we shall use IVb, since it produces a smoother bass part (the leap of a third instead of a fifth).

We can now add two more bass notes.

EXAMPLE 105

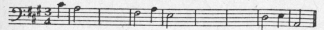

We now have six more chords to fill in. There are several alternative ways of completing the progression, so we work these out and hum or play them, mentally comparing the effects. Finally we decide on this bass part :

EXAMPLE 106

This is reasonably melodious and does not violate any rule of melodic progression. We can now add a soprano part. The third and fourth notes are both first inversions, so we may let the melody run in sixths with the bass. Having fixed on D for the third note of the melody, we can fill in the first two notes, A and C sharp, which lead naturally to it and also have the merit of moving in contrary motion with the bass. (Contrary motion between the soprano and bass parts should always be used when possible.) We may now complete the melody, letting each note proceed to the nearest note of the next chord, and carefully avoiding consecutive fifths and octaves.

EXAMPLE 107

All that now remains to be done is to fill in the alto and tenor parts. I leave you to do this as an exercise.

This may seem a laborious and somewhat mechanical method of composition, but it is simply a means to an end. The experienced composer would probably sketch out the soprano and bass parts, or all four parts, at the same time. He would, at any rate, have a clear idea of the harmony as a whole before he puts pen to paper. The beginner, before he can do this, must learn to hear melody and harmony simultaneously.

The best way to acquire this faculty, which is essential to the writing of intelligent harmony, is to take a passage in two- or four-part harmony and, by looking at it, try to realize its effect. When you have made up your mind, play the passage on the piano and test the accuracy of your impressions. All the examples in this book should be treated in this way ; a book of hymn tunes will provide additional exercises.

Meanwhile you can start simple composition on the lines carried out in this chapter. Before you do this make quite certain that you do really understand the principles outlined in previous chapters. If there is anything you have forgotten or failed to grasp, go over it again. Composition must be built on secure foundations ; it is simply a waste of time to put on paper anything that you cannot hear in your mind.

Exercises

Compose complete sentences, consisting of two four-bar phrases, on the lines indicated in this chapter. Use $\frac{2}{4}$, $\frac{3}{4}$ or $\frac{4}{4}$ time. Be careful to write each sentence in such a key that each harmony part lies within the compass of the voice for which it is written.

CHAPTER XI

MAJOR TRIADS (SECOND INVERSION)

In the second inversion of a Triad the fifth is in the bass, and the other two notes a sixth and a fourth above the bass ; it is therefore spoken of as the **Chord of the Six-Four.**

EXAMPLE 108

Ic

The use of the second inversion is much more restricted than that of the first, and for the time being we shall use it only on the Dominant note, resolving it on the root position of the chord on the same bass note.[1] This progression is called the **Cadential Six-Four** because it is frequently used at a cadence.

EXAMPLE 109

Ic   Va

This progression, when preceded by some other chord, produces a decorated form of Imperfect Cadence.

For the time being the second inversion should be preceded either by IVa (*see* Example 110), IVb (*see*

---

[1] The bass note may, of course, be either repeated, sustained or moved up or down an octave.

EXAMPLE 110

Imperfect Cadence   Decorated Form

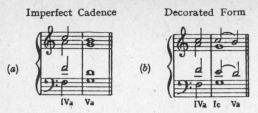

Example 111 (*a*)), Ia (*see* Example 111 (*b*)), or Ib (*see* Example 111 (*c*)).

This decorated Imperfect Cadence has the cadence chord (Va) on a weaker part of the bar, owing to the intrusion of the second inversion on the strong accent ; for this reason it is usually known as a " feminine ending." Play either of the decorated forms in Example 111, stopping on the second chord (Ic), and you will

EXAMPLE 111

notice that it seems to demand some other chord to follow it. Compare the two forms of cadence in Example 110 and you will find that the decorated form is the more flowing and persuasive.

The decorated Imperfect Cadence is used in the same way as the normal form (*i.e.* to end the middle phrase of a sentence). Play Example 111 and you will feel that although the cadence gives the effect of temporary rest, the flow of the music is not interrupted.

When the progression Ic Va is followed by Ia, a decorated form of Perfect Cadence is produced.

EXAMPLE 112

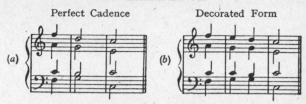

For the time being the second inversion in this cadence should be preceded either by IVa (*see* Example 112), IVb (*see* Example 113 (*a*)), or Ib (*see* Example 113 (*b*)). Ia should not be used as it would weaken the effect of the cadence chord.

EXAMPLE 113

The decorated Perfect Cadence is, of course, a very common musical idiom. A familiar example of its use may be found in the last two bars of *God Save the Queen*.

The following recommendations should be memorized.

(1) The best note to double in a second inversion is the bass note (*i.e.* the fifth of the Triad) ; see the examples in this chapter. The doubling of either of the other notes is generally unsatisfactory.

(2) To obtain a smooth progression between Ic and Va, the sixth and fourth (from the bass) of the first chord should fall to the fifth and third of the second chord (see the examples in this chapter).

(3) In a Cadential Six-Four, Ic should not be placed on a weaker beat than Va.

EXAMPLE 114

(4) When the soprano and bass notes of a second inversion are a perfect fourth apart, they should not be approached by similar motion.

EXAMPLE 115

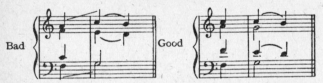

The Cadential Six-Four may be used with good effect (1) when the bass part pauses on the Dominant

EXAMPLE 116

note at a cadence (*see* Example 116 (*a*)) and (2) when the melody falls from the Tonic to the Leading Note (*see* Example 116 (*c*)), or from the Mediant to the Supertonic (*see* Example 116 (*b*)).

Before attempting the exercises which follow, make quite certain that you are able to distinguish (by ear and by eye) between the ordinary Perfect and Imperfect Cadences and those formed by the Cadential Six-Four. In addition to studying the examples in this chapter you should pick out (from any book of hymn tunes) a number of Cadential Six-Fours, carefully noting where they occur, and whether they conform to the principles outlined in this chapter.

Exercises

(1) By using the Cadential Six-Four convert the following ordinary cadences into decorated ones.

(2) Add alto, tenor, and bass parts to the following, introducing the Cadential Six-Four where appropriate :

(3) Add soprano, alto, and tenor parts to the following, introducing the Cadential Six-Four where appropriate :

(a)

(b)

(4) Compose complete sentences consisting of two four-bar phrases, and introducing the Cadential Six-Four.

CHAPTER XII

PRIMARY TRIADS IN THE MINOR KEY

Example 117 shows the Triads formed on the seven degrees of the Harmonic Minor Scale. This is the form of Minor Scale generally used in the construction of chords, and for the time being we shall consider it exclusively.

EXAMPLE 117
KEY OF C MINOR

You will see that the Tonic and Subdominant Triads are minor (instead of major), but that the Dominant Triad remains major (as in the major key). At the moment we are only concerned with the Primary Triads, but it should be noted in passing that the Mediant Triad is formed by placing above the root a major third and an augmented fifth ; it is therefore known as an **Augmented Triad**.

In a general way all the rules and recommendations relating to the Primary Triads in the major key apply

EXAMPLE 118

equally to those in the minor key. It is a simple matter to turn a progression in a major key into the key of its Tonic Minor, by changing the key signature and sharpening the Leading Note.

Play Example 118 and notice the mental effect of the change from major to minor—(*a*) bright and hopeful; (*b*) subdued and rather sad. The different characteristics of major and minor keys are discussed in a later chapter, and for the moment it is only necessary to point out that music in a minor key is generally (though by no means invariably) of a more sombre character than that in a major key.

In the Harmonic Minor Scale the interval of an augmented second occurs between the sixth and seventh degrees, and we know that this interval is forbidden by the laws of melodic progression. It is clear, then, that the sixth and seventh degrees must not be allowed to occur consecutively in the same part. Since we are restricted (for the moment) to the Primary Triads, this can only happen when IV is followed by V, or vice versa. In proceeding from IVa to Va the sixth degree of the scale should be approached from above.

EXAMPLE 119

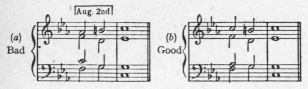

In Example 119 (*a*) the sixth degree *rises* to the seventh degree, thus producing a forbidden augmented second. In Example 119 (*b*) the sixth degree *falls* to the fifth, and the augmented second is therefore avoided.

When Va is followed by IVa, the seventh degree

should rise to the octave, and the sixth should be
approached from below. Compare (*a*) with (*b*) in the
example which follows.

EXAMPLE 120

It is obvious that IVb cannot be followed by Vb,
or vice versa, as the bass notes of the two chords would
form an augmented second. Write both chords out and
test this for yourself.

All other progressions which are satisfactory in the
major key may also be used in the minor, so long as
augmented intervals are avoided. Play over the
examples in Chapters VII, IX, and XI, transposing them
from the major key to that of the Tonic Minor, and you
will find that with the exception of Example 100 (consecutive first inversions of IV and V), they are all
equally good in the minor key.

The third of a Minor Triad (*e.g.* I or IV in the minor
key) may be doubled if there is sufficient reason for doing
so, but for the time being it is best to double the root
of a chord in root position, and the root or fifth of a first
inversion.

Exercises

(1) Add parts for alto and tenor.

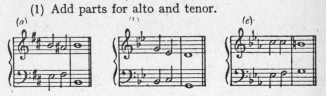

(2) Write the following progressions in four-part harmony, in the keys indicated :

(a) C Minor.	Ia	Ib	Va	Ia
(b) F Minor.	IVa	Ic	Va	Ia
(c) D Minor.	Ia	IVa	Va	Ia
(d) G Minor.	Ia	Ib	IVa	Va

(3) Play on the piano, in four-part harmony, Perfect, Imperfect, and Plagal Cadences in the following minor keys : G, C, A, D, F, B, F sharp.

(4) Add parts for alto, tenor, and bass.

(5) Add parts for soprano, alto, and tenor.

(6) Transpose the melody (or bass part) given in the following exercises from the Major to the Tonic Minor key, adding the parts as directed.

(a) Chapter IX, 3.   (b) Chapter XI, 2(a).
(c) Chapter XI, 3(a).

CHAPTER XIII

THE CHORD OF THE DOMINANT SEVENTH

So far we have only considered chords consisting of three different notes, one of which must be doubled in four-part harmony. There are, however, many chords containing four or more different notes, which are used by composers to give variety and interest to their music.

We have seen that a Triad is formed by placing above a root two notes a third and a fifth from it. If we add a fourth note a seventh above the root, we form what is known as a **Chord of the Seventh.** This chord may occur on any degree of the Major or Minor Scale, but the most useful Chord of the Seventh (and the only one we shall consider for the moment) is that formed on the Dominant.

If we place above the Dominant Triad a note a minor seventh from the root, we form the chord of the **Dominant Seventh.**

EXAMPLE 121

V7

Example 121 shows the Dominant Seventh in the key of C; it is figured V_7 to distinguish it from the Dominant Triad. Play it on the piano and you will feel that its chief characteristic is an urgent desire for resolution. This is because the three upper notes form a Diminished Triad, and, as we have seen, the effect of the dissonant diminished fifth is incomplete until it is resolved. If you experiment with the diminished fifth you will find that the most satisfactory way of resolving it is to let the Leading Note rise to the Tonic, and the Subdominant fall to the Mediant, thus :

EXAMPLE 122

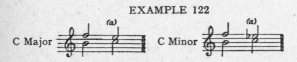

Since the notes at (a), together with the root of the Dominant Seventh (G), form the Tonic Triad of C, it follows that V_7 may be satisfactorily resolved on I. This, in fact, is by far the most usual resolution.[1]

EXAMPLE 123

V7   I

As the Dominant Seventh consists of four different notes, three inversions are possible. Example 124 shows (a) the first inversion, with the third in the bass ; (b) the second inversion, with the fifth in the bass ; and (c) the third inversion (figured V_7d), with the seventh in the bass.

EXAMPLE 124

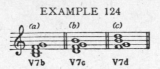

V7b   V7c   V7d

---

[1] Observe that the Dominant Seventh is identical in both the Major and Minor Key.

The root position of the Dominant Seventh may be used instead of the Dominant Triad at a Perfect Cadence or a Cadential Six-Four ; the effect is equally conclusive.

EXAMPLE 125

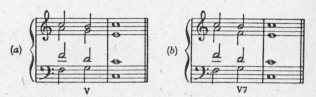

The inversions of the Dominant Seventh may be used freely during the course of a phrase.[1]

EXAMPLE 126

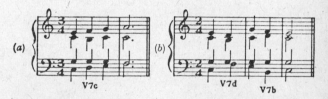

The appropriate use of the inversions imparts a certain flexibility to a progression of chords. Observe that the consecutive fifths in Example 126 (*a*) (between the soprano and alto parts, in the second and third chords) are not objectionable because the first fifth is diminished and the second perfect. It is only consecutive *perfect* fifths which are ugly.

---

[1] The opening bars of Beethoven's *Sonata Pathétique* are based on the chord progression shown in Example 126 (*b*).

The Dominant Seventh may often be used effectively on a half beat between V and I (*see* Example 127).

EXAMPLE 127

The inversions may also be used in Inverted Cadences.

EXAMPLE 128

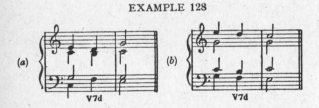

Example 128 shows two such Inverted Cadences, the second a form of the Cadential Six-Four. The value of Inverted Cadences is that they preserve the flow of the music. Dr. Crotch (1775–1847) once defined composition as " the art of avoiding Full Closes." Music which is constantly being checked by Full Closes is as discomforting to the listener as a fidgety rider to a spirited horse.

You have now a sufficiently wide choice of chords to enable you to keep your harmony moving. Experiment with Inverted Cadences, Inverted Dominant Sevenths,

and Inverted Triads ; find out how other composers
use them, and how they contribute to the shape and
proportion of music.   Almost any one, with practice
and patience, may learn to use chords and cadences
correctly ; your task is to use them *imaginatively*.

In the inversions of the Dominant Seventh all four
notes should usually be present, no note being doubled
in four-part harmony.   When V₇a is followed by Ia
the fifth may be omitted from V₇a and the root doubled

EXAMPLE 129

Alternatively the fifth may be omitted from Ia
(*see* Example 123).   The third and the seventh, being the
characteristic notes of the chord, should not be left out.

The following rules of progression should be
memorized.

(1) The third of the Dominant Seventh should
normally rise one step to the Tonic, and the seventh fall
one step to the Mediant (*see* Example 123).   When V7c
is followed by Ib (*see* Example 126 (*a*)) the seventh may
rise one step to the Dominant.

(2) In the inversions the bass note should usually
be quitted by step (*see* Examples 127 and 128), but the
bass note may sometimes leap to another position of the
same chord.

(3) The seventh may rise to the root, or fall to the fifth, before resolution (*i.e.* the chord may change from V₇ to V), so long as it is correctly resolved as soon as the Dominant harmony changes.

EXAMPLE 130

Exercises

N.B.—In harmonizing a given bass part the following chords are now available :

Bass Note	Chord
Tonic	Ia
Supertonic	V₇c
Mediant	Ib
Subdominant	IVa or V₇d
Dominant	Va or V₇a
Submediant	IVb
Leading Note	Vb or V₇b

(1) Play (and write) the root position and inversions of the Dominant Seventh in all major and minor keys, resolving them on the Tonic Triad, thus :

(2) Write the following progressions in four-part harmony, in the keys indicated.

(a) Key B flat Major   Ia   IVb V₇b Ia

(b) Key G Minor   Ia   IVa V₇d Ib

(c) Key F Major   IVa Ic   V₇a Ia

(d) Key A Major   Ib   IVa V₇a Ia

(e) Key C Minor   IVa Ib V₇c Ia

(3) Add parts for alto, tenor, and bass.

(a)

(b)

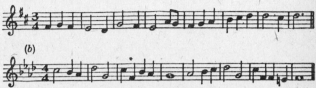

(4) Add parts for soprano, alto, and tenor.

(a)

(b)

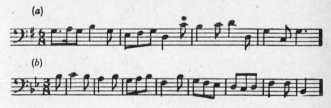

---

* The bass part here leaps a minor seventh; this leap is quite good if the part moves from one position of a chord to another (for this purpose V and V7 may be regarded as the same chord).

CHAPTER XIV

SOME SECONDARY TRIADS

The Secondary Triads occur on the second, third, sixth and seventh degrees of the Major or Minor Scale. The Mediant and Leading Note Triads require special treatment, and for the present we shall only consider the Triads formed on the Supertonic and the Submediant.

The Primary Triads form, so to speak, a family circle into which the introduction of distant or near relations—the Secondary Triads—often affords a welcome break from a too familiar routine.

The Supertonic Triad

The Supertonic Triad, which is perhaps the most useful of all the Secondary Triads, usually leads up to one of the Primary Triads. One of the most natural and valuable progressions is from the Supertonic to the Dominant Triad ; this forms a new kind of Imperfect Cadence, and a useful approach either to the Perfect Cadence, or Cadential Six-Four.

EXAMPLE 131

Example 131 shows (a) an Imperfect Cadence in the major key ; (b) a Perfect Cadence in the major key (this may also be taken in the minor key) ; (c) a Cadential Six-Four in the minor key (this may also be taken in the major key).

In major keys the Supertonic Triad is minor ; in minor keys it is diminished. A Diminished Triad is very rarely used in root position as the effect is usually unsatisfactory. In the minor key only the first inversion of the Supertonic Triad should therefore be used ; in the major key either the root position or the first inversion is satisfactory. (For the present the second inversion of a Triad should only be used in the Cadential Six-Four ; other uses are left over for future treatment.)

You will see from Example 131 (b) and (c) that the bass note of IIb may be doubled with good effect. In a first inversion of a minor Triad it is often good to double the third of the chord instead of the root (see page 103), and in the first inversion of a Diminished Triad it is usually best to double the root.

The recommendations so far given as to doubling in first inversions may be summarized thus :

(1) In the first inversion of a **major** Triad double either the root or the fifth of the chord.

(2) In the first inversion of a **minor** Triad double the root or the third[1] (especially in IIb).

(3) In the first inversion of a **diminished** Triad double the third.

The Supertonic Triad is effective when preceded by the Subdominant Triad (see Example 131 (a)), or by the Submediant Triad (see Example 134 (a)), but less effective when preceded by the Dominant Triad. When it is preceded or followed by the Tonic Triad, one or both chords should be in the first inversion ; the effect of Ia IIa, or vice versa, is seldom good.

---

[1] i.e. the bass note.

The Submediant Triad

In major keys the Submediant Triad is minor ; in minor keys it is major. This chord is most useful in root position, although the first inversion may be freely used.

When the Dominant Chord (Triad or Seventh) is followed by the Submediant Triad, a new kind of cadence is formed.

EXAMPLE 132

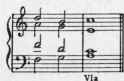

VIa

The Dominant Triad in Example 132 suggests a Perfect Cadence, but instead of the expected Tonic Triad the ear is surprised by the appearance of the Submediant Triad. The cadence formed by the two chords V VI is known as an **Interrupted** Cadence. Like the Imperfect Cadence this gives the effect of rest without finality, and may be used as an intermediate, but not a final, cadence.[1] The Interrupted Cadence may be preceded by the Supertonic Triad (*see* Example 132), the Subdominant Triad, or the Tonic Triad ; a familiar example of its use is found in the fourth bar of *God Save the Queen*, where it is preceded by the Tonic Triad (*see* Example 133).

EXAMPLE 133

VIa

---

[1] *See* page 79.

The second chord of the first bar of Example 133 illustrates another use of the Submediant Triad ; when harmonizing the Tonic and Mediant degrees of the scale, the Submediant Triad may often be used as an alternative to the Tonic Triad.

The Submediant Triad may be used to precede the Supertonic Triad (*see* Example 134 (*a*)), the Dominant Triad, when both chords are in root position (*see* Example 134 (*b*)), the Cadential Six-Four (*see* Example 134 (*c*)), and all other cadences except the Interrupted Cadence.

EXAMPLE 134

VIa   IIa   VIa   Va   VIa   Ic   Va

The progressions in Example 133 and 134 are equally good in the minor key, with the exception of Example 134 (*a*) in which the Supertonic Triad appears in root position. Example 131 (*a*) is ineffective in the minor key for the same reason.

In all the examples in this chapter[1] the third of the Submediant Triad is doubled. In the major key this is generally desirable, and in the minor key, when Va is followed by VIa (or vice versa), it is imperative.

The Supertonic and Submediant Triads should be used sparingly at the moment, along the lines indicated in this chapter, as their indiscriminate use tends to confuse the tonality of the music.

---

[1] Except Example 134(*a*)

The following general recommendations on the use of Triads should be carefully studied before the exercises are attempted.

(1) Progressions from a Triad in root position to another Triad in root position are generally better when the root falls rather than rises a third.

EXAMPLE 135

(a) Good   (b) Poor

(2) Progressions from a Triad in root position to another Triad in root position are generally good when the root rises or falls a fourth or fifth. But Va to IIa is seldom good.

(3) The first inversion of a Secondary Triad generally sounds best when the highest note is a sixth from the bass, and when the bass is quitted by step.

Exercises

(1) Write (and play) the following progressions in four-part harmony, in the keys indicated :—

    (a) Key A Major   Ib   IVa IIa Va Ia
    (b) Key C Minor   Ia   V7a Ib IVa IIb V7a Ia
    (c) Key G Major   Ia   IVa Ib V7c Ia Va VIa
    (d) Key D Minor   Ia   V7c Ib VIa Ic Va Ia

(2) Play on the piano in various major and minor keys (a) Interrupted Cadences, (b) Perfect and Imperfect Cadences, and (c) Cadential Six-Fours, preceded by II or VI.

(3) Add parts for alto, tenor, and bass, introducing Secondary Triads where appropriate.

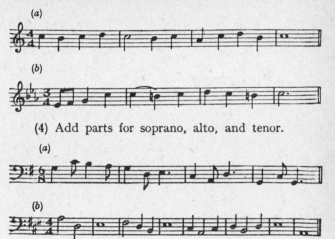

(4) Add parts for soprano, alto, and tenor.

CHAPTER XV

PASSING NOTES

Up to the present we have harmonized each note of a melody with a separate chord. Hymn and psalm tunes are generally treated in this way, but if you take up a piano piece, or a song, you will find that some of the melody notes move up and down the scale above a single sustained chord.

EXAMPLE 136

In Example 136 the notes marked with asterisks do not belong to the harmony, but are dissonant notes passing between one harmony note and another. They are therefore called **Passing Notes**. You will see that (a) is simply a decorated form of (b).

Passing notes add grace and freedom to melody. If each melody note in Example 136 (a) were harmonized with a separate chord the effect would be stiff and cumbrous if the music were quick and light, though it might be satisfactory at a more dignified pace.

Essential Notes

Since passing notes do not form part of the chord against which they are sounded they are often called

unessential notes, whereas those notes which do belong
to the chord are called **essential.** In the second bar of
Example 136 (*a*) only the second melody note is unessential, since the first and third notes both belong to
the harmony.

EXAMPLE 137

In Example 137 there are no passing notes. The
melody notes in the second bar are all essential notes of
the same chord ; in the first bar the harmony moves
from the Dominant Triad to the third inversion of the
Dominant Seventh (*see* page 107).

Essential notes in two or more parts may change
position at the same time.

EXAMPLE 138

Care must be taken to avoid forbidden consecutives.
In Example 138 (*a*) had the tenor part held the note B
instead of moving to D consecutive octaves would have
resulted between the soprano and tenor parts ; in
addition the second chord would have had a doubled
third, but no fifth.

Auxiliary and Changing Notes

A passing (*i.e.* unessential) note may either return to the harmony note from which it started (as in Example 139) or pass on to a new note.

EXAMPLE 139

A passing note which returns to the harmony note from which it started is called an **auxiliary** note. Example 139 shows auxiliary notes (*a*) below the harmony notes, and (*b*) above the harmony notes.

An auxiliary note may sometimes leap a third to another auxiliary note and then return either to the harmony note or to some other note of the chord. These are called **changing** notes.

EXAMPLE 140

Example 140 illustrates three kinds of changing notes.

(*a*) Consists of the harmony note, the note above, the note below, and the harmony note; (*b*) and (*d*) consist of the harmony note, the note below, the note above, and the harmony note.

The first and fourth notes of (c) are both harmony notes of the same chord. The second and third notes are auxiliary notes, each below the respective harmony note.

An auxiliary note used below the harmony note is usually a semitone distant ;[1] used above the harmony note it is usually the next note of the Diatonic Scale (Major or Minor). This is by no means invariable ; the ear must judge whether a semitone or a tone gives the better effect in any particular context.

Passing Notes

Passing notes may be used on the beat, when they are called **accented** passing notes,[2] or after the beat, when they are called **unaccented** passing notes. Passing notes moving in thirds or sixths may occur in two parts simultaneously, or, more rarely, in thirds and sixths together in the three upper parts. These and other uses are illustrated in Example 141, which should be carefully studied.

EXAMPLE 141

[1] When the harmony note is the major third of the scale, the auxiliary note may be either a semitone or a tone below it.

[2] The accented passing note (also known as the **Appogiatura**) by bringing the dissonance into prominence thereby heightens the interest of the listener. This feeling of intensity or stress should be compared with the less pungent effect of the unaccented passing note.

(*a*) and (*b*) are auxiliary notes doubled in sixths between the soprano and tenor parts. Observe that at (*b*) the auxiliary note is a tone below the harmony note. This auxiliary note could be sharpened if desired, so as to be a semitone below the harmony note ; the choice of either interval is simply a matter of taste.

EXAMPLE 142

But observe that if the upper auxiliary note is a semitone below the harmony note, the lower auxiliary note must be at the same distance. Thus in Example 142 if the third note of the soprano part is sharpened the tenor part must follow suit.

(*c*), (*f*), (*g*) and (*h*) are accented passing notes. The effect of an accented passing note is generally better if the note on which it resolves is not doubled in any of the upper parts ; it may, however, be doubled in the bass.

(*d*) is an example of the same (unaccented) passing note occurring in two parts simultaneously. This is only good when the two parts move in contrary motion.

(*e*) shows auxiliary notes, moving in thirds and sixths together, occurring simultaneously in three upper parts. This is only effective when the three upper parts move in close position while the bass remains stationary.

Anticipations

Example 140 (*e*) shows yet another kind of passing note. The semiquaver in the melody is called an

EXAMPLE 143

anticipation because it moves to the note of the next chord before the harmony has changed. The anticipation is mostly used to anticipate the final note of a cadence, but it may also occur during the course of a phrase,[1] the note anticipated being either essential or unessential. The anticipation generally appears in the melody.

Example 143 (a)[2] shows the anticipation of an unessential note; Example 143 (b) the anticipation of an essential note.

When two harmony notes are a step apart, as in Example 143 (c), (d) and (e), the unessential note above the first harmony note may leap down a third to the second harmony note.

Except in the above circumstances, or in changing notes, a passing note should be quitted by step; in the early stages it is best to approach it by step also, though when experience has been gained this restriction may often be relaxed.

---

[1] Well-known instances of anticipations occur in *Home, Sweet Home* and in Victor Herbert's *Ah, Sweet Mystery of Life*.

[2] The third of the chord is doubled at the start so that it will be present when the melody falls to the tonic.

Chromatic Passing Notes

Chromatic, as well as diatonic, passing notes may be used.

EXAMPLE 144

You will see that the melody in Example 144 is based on the Chromatic Scale of C Major. When a chromatic passing note is introduced it is best to let the part proceed in semitones until the next harmony note is reached. Chromatic passing notes, which are rather more difficult to handle than diatonic, should be used very sparingly at the moment. They are more often used in instrumental than in vocal music.

Passing Notes in the Minor Key

In the minor key care must be taken to avoid the interval of an augmented second between the sixth and seventh degrees of the Harmonic Minor Scale. When both the sixth and seventh degrees are passing notes (as in Example 145 (*a*)) the Melodic Minor Scale is generally used (*i.e.* major in ascending, minor in descending). When the minor sixth of the scale is a harmony

EXAMPLE 145

note and the seventh a passing note (as in Example
145 (*b*)) the minor seventh is used. When the Leading
Note of the scale is the harmony note and the sixth the
passing note (as in Example 145 (*c*)) the major sixth is
used.

General Recommendations

(1) When two passing notes move by step in the
same direction it is better to let the second note continue
in that direction than return to the first note.

EXAMPLE 146

The first bar of Example 136, in which this recommendation is carried out, is better than Example 146,
in which the second passing note returns to the first.

(2) A passing note should pass forwards or back-
wards ; it should not remain to become a new harmony
note. Thus Example 147 is bad because the lower
passing note remains to become the fifth of the new chord.

EXAMPLE 147

(3) Passing notes will not make an unsatisfactory
progression (*e.g.* one in which forbidden consecutives
occur) into a satisfactory one ; but they may, if care-

lessly employed, cause faults in an otherwise good progression.

The Application of Passing Notes

It is clear that with the means now at our disposal a melody may be harmonized in several different ways. We may harmonize each note with a separate chord, or we may treat certain melody notes as passing notes, and harmonize two or more with a single chord. In deciding the kind of harmony most suited to a particular melody both the character and the pace of the music must be taken into consideration. In Example 148 a melody is harmonized with two chords, Tonic and Dominant. This very simple harmonization has a quiet, contemplative effect which might be well suited to a lullaby, or some other gentle piece of music performed at a moderate pace.

EXAMPLE 148

In Example 149 the same melody is harmonized with five chords instead of two. This harmonization is

EXAMPLE 149

less tender but more virile than the previous example, and would be better at a slower pace.

In Example 150 the character of the melody is still further changed, each note being harmonized with a separate chord. This effect is obviously much stronger than that of the two previous examples, but what it gains in vitality it loses in delicacy and charm. This example would be better at a slower pace than the others. But it must be repeated that the character as well as the pace of the music must be considered, and that all three examples could quite well be played at the same speed, though the effect of each would be different.

EXAMPLE 150

It is not possible to offer more than general observations on the best method of harmonizing any particular melody ; it is largely a question of the individual taste, and imaginative powers of thinking and hearing, of the composer.

You will see that in Examples 148 and 149 the first note of the melody is not harmonized. When a melody begins on a portion of a bar, this portion is frequently left unharmonized. During the course of a phrase it is by no means essential that every melody note should be harmonized.

EXAMPLE 151

The First Violet.   MENDELSSOHN

Except in hymn tunes, and similar music in which each melody note is usually harmonized, the occasional introduction of rests, or of silent beats or bars, prevents the musical structure from becoming stodgy and monotonous.   "A piece of music," wrote Sir Charles Stanford[1] (1852–1924), "has to breathe like a human being; the rests are the breathing places."   In a future chapter we shall see how variety of texture may be obtained by varying the number of harmony parts.   The exercises in this chapter are still to be worked in four parts, but in harmonizing melodies we shall " let in the air " now and then, by leaving certain portions unharmonized.

In Example 151 we have only three chords to thirteen melody notes ;   yet the harmony remains clear cut. Play this example and you will find that the melody suggests harmony even where it is not harmonized ; the first five notes strongly suggest Dominant harmony in the key of F Minor, and the next two notes suggest Tonic harmony even before the Tonic Chord is struck Notice, too, how the syncopated chords in the second bar fill out the rhythm.   Play this example again, transferring these two chords to the accented (first and third) beats of the bar, and observe how the effect is weakened.

---

[1] *Musical Composition* (Macmillan).

Exercises

1. Add unessential notes where appropriate, distributing them among the different voices as far as possible.

Start thus :

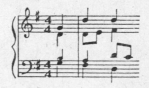

2. Rewrite Examples 140 and 141, removing all unessential notes.

3. Harmonize the following melodies in four parts, using unessential notes where appropriate. Give the music " breathing space " by leaving some notes of each melody unharmonized.

(a) Moderato

(b)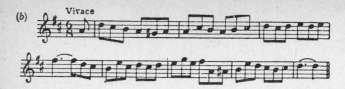

Start (*a*) thus :

Start (*b*) thus :

CHAPTER XVI

WRITING FOR THE PIANO

So far we have regarded all music as being written in four parts for voices, the principles of four-part vocal writing being the foundations upon which all harmony is built. The time has now come to consider the different mediums through which music may be presented, beginning with the piano.

It is clear that the treatment of piano music must differ considerably from that of vocal music. The combined compass of all four voices (soprano, alto, tenor and bass) is little more than three octaves, whereas the usual compass of a modern piano is seven. Four voices can make only four different sounds at the same time, whereas the pianist can produce at least ten, and can indulge in distant skips and intervals which would be quite inadmissible in vocal music. The singer is able to sustain a sound at constant power, or swell and diminish it, but the sound of a piano string decreases until it dies away. There is also a difference of tone-quality and technique.

The composer who has not at least an elementary knowledge of piano playing is obviously at a disadvantage when writing for the piano, but much may be done by the study of piano music ; books of graded piano studies[1] are particularly helpful, since each study usually illustrates some different point of technique. If, in addition, a piece of music which is to be played on the radio or the gramophone is intelligently studied beforehand, the

---

[1] *The Hundred Best From Czerny* (Paterson) may be recommended for this purpose.

accuracy of the impressions may be checked by following the score during performance. Nevertheless, actual experimentation at the keyboard is the most valuable of all exercises, since the capabilities and limitations of the instrument are then brought home by personal experience. Without this experience the composer may well write passages which are ineffective, or even impossible to execute.

Although no written instructions can take the place of actual demonstration, the points which follow will show the beginner what to look for in studying piano technique. Piano music is written on two staves;[1] normally the upper stave is in the treble clef and is played by the right hand, and the lower stave is in the bass clef and is played by the left hand. When certain notes are either too high or too low to be written conveniently in the usual clef, the clefs are sometimes temporarily interchanged, the right hand playing in the bass clef, or the left hand in the treble clef. Occasionally, to save a change of clef, a right hand passage is placed on the lower stave, or a left hand passage on the upper stave, the notes to be played by each hand being distinguished by turning one set of tails up and the other set down. Where doubt might still exist the letters R.H. (Right Hand) or L.H. (Left Hand) are used. These points are exemplified in Examples 153 and 157.

No more than five notes can normally be played simultaneously with either hand. An exception is shown in Example 152 where six notes are played by the right hand, the two adjacent white notes joined by the square bracket being taken with the thumb. But this use is comparatively rare, and even Example 152 would

---

[1] Exceptionally on three staves.

EXAMPLE 152

be better if the seventh (G) were not doubled in the upper octave.

When several notes are to be played simultaneously by the fingers of one hand, the distance between the extreme notes should not exceed an octave, or a ninth[1] at most. There may, however, be a wide gap between the hands, and the music may leap freely from one octave to another, as in Example 153.

EXAMPLE 153

Bagatelle. BEETHOVEN, Op. 33, No. 7

---

[1] Observe that the left hand part in Example 152 must be played by passing the first finger over the thumb, the lower A being sustained by means of the damper pedal.

The Use of the Pedals

By depressing the damper (right hand) pedal[1] chords may be played which are too widely spaced to be sustained by the fingers alone. Example 154 shows several chords (taken from the piano works of Lizst) which may be played in this way.

EXAMPLE 154

In Example 154 (*a*) the notes of the left hand chord are spread (*i.e.* played in rapid succession from the bottom note upwards), the damper pedal being depressed as the first note is played, so that each note is sustained as it is sounded. Notice the overlapping of the hands, a device often useful in piano writing. In Example 154 (*c*) and (*d*) the notes in both hands are spread. In Example 154 (*b*) the small notes in the left hand are first played in rapid succession, and the main chord is then played in the usual way, the damper pedal being held down throughout.[2]

---

[1] The damper pedal, when depressed, raises all the dampers from the strings, so that any notes which have been sounded continue to sound, even though the keys are released, until the dampers are lowered or the vibrations of the strings come to an end. Its use is shown by the sign " Ped," and its release by *. The upper strings, having no dampers, are not affected by the pedal.

[2] The use of the damper pedal *enriches* the sound, for when one string is set in vibration with the dampers raised, all the other strings are free to vibrate in sympathy with it.

The use of the soft pedal[1] should only be indicated when a special kind of tone-colour is wanted—this may be described as "silvery" but should be tested by experiment. The soft pedal may be used independently of the damper pedal, or both pedals may be used together.

Tone-colour

Example 153 shows how the different registers of the piano may be contrasted effectively. A few minutes at the keyboard will reveal the difference in tone-colour better than any description. Observe that a chord in a lower octave is more weighty than one in a higher octave, and that a widely spaced chord has a lighter but less brilliant effect than a chord in close position. Broadly speaking the middle five octaves are the most generally useful, the highest and lowest octaves being reserved for special effects. The pitch of the two lowest octaves is rather indefinite, and it is usually better to place the notes of a chord at least a fifth apart in the lowest octave but one, and at least an octave apart in the lowest octave.

Harmony in Piano Music

It is clear from the preceding examples that piano chords are not restricted to four parts. The number usually varies considerably during the course of a movement. Thus Example 155 starts in five parts, then goes to four, three, and finally two.

---

[1] The use of the soft pedal is shown by the words *Una Corda* and its release by *Tre Corda*.

EXAMPLE 155

The number of notes in a chord is conditioned by (*a*) the need for arranging the harmonies so that they lie easily under the hands, and (*b*) the musical effect required. Harmony in seven or eight parts is much fuller and richer than that in three or four ; when a brilliant *forte* effect is desired, therefore, the number of parts are frequently increased.

In general the rules of four-part harmony should be observed, but it will be helpful, before going further, to consider in what respects the treatment of harmony in fewer or more than four parts differs from that of four-part harmony.

Harmony in Three and Two Parts

In three-part writing all three notes of a Triad should be present when possible, but to avoid consecutives it is often necessary to omit the fifth and double the root (as in the second chord of Example 156). In the first inversion of a Triad the root may occasionally be omitted, and the fifth doubled. In chords of more than three notes, the characteristic notes should be retained (*e.g.* in the Dominant Seventh the third and seventh should be kept and the fifth omitted, as in the third chord of Example 156).

In three-part writing a succession of first inversions may be used without restriction so long as the root is placed in the top part (*see* Example 155) ; the rule for

EXAMPLE 156

the alternate doubling of the root and the fifth in four-part harmony[1] does not apply.

In two-part writing at least one note of every chord must necessarily be omitted, so that it is only possible to suggest the harmony by means of skeleton chords. On the rare occasions when it is desirable to introduce two-part writing it is best to use consonant intervals (chiefly thirds and sixths), with an occasional dissonant interval correctly approached and resolved. Unisons and octaves are best confined to the first and last notes of a passage, and should never be used consecutively unless, of course,

EXAMPLE 157

Rustic Dance. MENDELSSOHN

[1]*See* page 87.

the whole passage moves in unison or octaves, when it becomes, in effect, one-part writing. Fifths should be used very sparingly except when a characteristic effect is wanted, as in Example 157. Two-part writing may be freely duplicated in another octave, as in the last two bars of Example 157.

Harmony in more than Four Parts

In writing chords in five or more parts the rules given for four-part harmonic progression should be observed as far as possible, although these rules are more and more relaxed as the number of parts is increased. In five-part harmony any note of a Triad may be doubled except the leading-note; in the chord of the dominant seventh it is usually best to double either the root or the fifth. In six or more parts any note, including the Leading Note, may generally be doubled, but in the Dominant Seventh it is best to avoid doubling the seventh.

EXAMPLE 158

Harmonic Progression

In piano music the bass is frequently doubled in octaves to strengthen its effect. Thus in Example 158(a) the writing is actually in four parts only, the addition of the lower octave to the bass notes merely strengthens them without adding any new parts to the harmony. Notes which lie between such octaves may also be doubled, as in Example 158 (b).

One or more of the higher parts may be doubled in octaves, as in Example 158 (c), but a higher part should not double the bass (Example 158 (d)) unless all the parts move together in octaves, as in Example 158 (e)).

Progressions such as the following :—

EXAMPLE 159
CHOPIN

are frequently to be found in piano music. The consecutive fifths in each hand are unobjectionable since both chords would be heard as a whole, the exact movement of the inner parts being undetected.

Similarly in this progression :—

EXAMPLE 160
Mazurka in F Minor. CHOPIN, Op. 7, No. 3

the consecutive fifths in the left hand are unobjectionable, being used to obtain a special effect of tone colour.
The spread chords in this example remind one of the
thrumming of a guitar.

Arpeggios and Broken Chords

The notes of a chord may be written in arpeggiated
or broken form[1] (*i.e.* to be sounded successively instead
of simultaneously).   These are characteristic idioms in
piano writing, and if properly laid out may easily be
performed at a considerable speed.   They appear in many

EXAMPLE 161

different forms, some of which are based on four-part
harmony.   The example which follows shows some of the
ways in which a simple progression may be decorated.

Arpeggios and broken chords such as the above are
only good when the progression of chords from which
they originate is satisfactory.   Thus Example 162 (*a*) is
bad because the progression from which it originates
(*b*) contains ugly consecutive octaves and fifths.

---

[1] The notes of an arpeggio are sounded in order, and those
of a broken chord out of order.   Thus the notes of a Triad on C
might be sounded in arpeggiated form as C E G C, and in broken
form as C G E C.

EXAMPLE 162

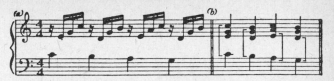

Arpeggios may be spread over a wide compass, as in Example 163. When played without the damper pedal the effect is harp-like ; with the damper pedal held down throughout, the effect is that of a sustained chord gradually built up.

EXAMPLE 163

Liszt

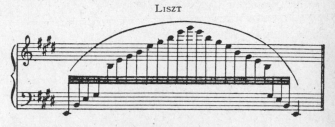

Melody and Accompaniment

A good proportion of piano writing takes the form of a melody with accompaniment, as in Example 164.

EXAMPLE 164

Tales from the Vienna Woods. JOHANN STRAUSS

Here the melody is the only really independent part. This form of accompaniment is extensively used in waltz music, and a similar form in marches and light piano pieces. The bass note, though sounded only on the first beat of the bar, must be considered as lasting throughout the bar, and resolved correctly upon the next bass note. This is perhaps a rather obvious point, but I have known beginners who have mistaken the F on the second beat of the first bar for the bass note of a second inversion, instead of an inner part.

Similarly, the real bass note of an arpeggio lasts in effect until the next bass note is sounded, and must therefore be changed when the harmony is changed. Example 165 (*a*) requires the addition of a new bass note on the second and fourth beats (as in Example 165 (*b*)), otherwise the bass notes sounded on the first and third beats will last in effect throughout the half bar, and give the undesired impression of second inversions.

EXAMPLE 165

The melody need not be confined to the top part, but may appear in any part, including the bass. In Example 166 the melody is in an inner part, with arpeggio accompaniment above it.

In this example the melody notes are played by each hand alternately ; this is simply a matter of convenience (as you will realize if you will play the passage over). Since the damper pedal is indicated the

EXAMPLE 166

Liebestraum. LISZT

bass note in each bar will sound throughout the bar, although only written as a crotchet. Later in this piece the melody appears in the top part with an arpeggio accompaniment beneath it.

EXAMPLE 167

The treble chords in the lower stave are played by the left hand which temporarily crosses over the right, a device which is often very effective.

In the next example the melody appears in the bass.

EXAMPLE 168

The Merry Peasant. SCHUMANN

From this example it is clear that the real bass of the harmony may sometimes appear in a higher part ; the last chord, for instance, is actually the Triad of F Major in root position, the real bass note appearing in the lowest part of the right-hand chord.

Unessential melody notes, clashing with an arpeggio or repeated chord accompaniment (*e.g.* A♮ against B♭ in Example 169 (*a*), and D♯ against D♮ in Example 169 (*b*)) are unobjectionable.

EXAMPLE 169

Observe that in the second bar of Example 169 (*b*) the bass moves from the root to the fifth of the Triad. This is a very common idiom in light piano music, and is used to avoid the repetition of the root ; this is often desirable in such music, as the harmony is usually of the simplest kind. Although the second chord of this bar is a second inversion it has no cadential significance when used in this way. Similarly, in the first bar of the same example, the bass moves from the third to the root of the Dominant Seventh.

Another common idiom is shown in Example 170. Though hackneyed it is not easy to avoid in certain forms of light music, as a glance at any collections of waltzes or marches will show. The inversions, occurring on a weak part of the bar, are merely decorative, the effect being virtually that of the Tonic Triad in root position throughout.[1]

---

[1] This idiom is sometimes taken in ascending, instead of descending, form.

EXAMPLE 170

Characteristic Piano Effects

Since music examples are to some extent ambiguous when separated from their contexts, I propose to illustrate some of the possible ways in which piano music may be arranged by analysing certain bars of an easily accessible piece—Johann Strauss's *Roses from the South* Waltzes. The effects described should be carefully noted, and compared with similar effects in other piano solos. The bars of the Introduction, and of the different waltzes, are counted separately (*i.e.* each starts from bar 1).

Introduction

Bars 1 to 6. A rich effect is obtained by doubling the melody in octaves in a lower part.

Bars 11 to 13. The melody is effectively accompanied by detached chords. Notice that the melody and accompaniment are some distance apart ; it is often extremely effective to separate them in this way.

Bars 17 to 20. The melody is doubled in octaves, with harmony notes in between (*i.e.* it is in three real parts) ; note the full effect.

Bar 24. The *tremolo* effect in the left hand, produced by the rapid reiteration of two different notes (or parts of the same chord) lends excitement to the music. It is a useful effect when not overdone.

Waltz 1

Bars 2 and 4. The melody is in two parts. Many similar examples will be found in these waltzes. Two-part writing, the principles of which have already been outlined, should, as far as possible, make satisfactory harmony when played with the bass only (*i.e.* with the accompaniment omitted). This also applies to melody in three or four parts.

Bars 5 to 7. The melody is in the top part, doubled in octaves.

Bars 25 to 38. The melody is in the top part, accompanied by broken chord figures in right hand and repeated chords in left. In bar 26 notice that B in first left-hand chord is changed to D in second, to avoid doubling the Leading Note.

Waltz 2

Bars 1 to 4. The melody is in octaves in the right hand, with accompanying chords between the octaves. Notice that the lower octave in the bass is written as a quaver; this gives a light effect comparable to the *pizzicato* (plucked string) of the double-bass.

Bars 17 to 20. Bars 1 to 4 are here repeated *forte* in a different form. The melody is in octaves with accompanying chords between the octaves, but an octave higher than in the previous example; the arpeggio accompaniment in the left hand gives added brilliance. When a melody is repeated it is frequently advisable to vary the treatment so as to avoid monotony.

Bar 48. Note the effective use of the trill (the rapid alternation of a given note with the note above). A trill generally ends with a turn, as in this example.

Waltz 3

Bars 5 to 8. The melody is doubled in thirds and octaves together, often a very effective device. The rest of the melody is doubled in thirds without the lower octave.

Waltz 4

Bars 10 to 12. The melody is doubled in sixths.

Bars 19 to 20. Note the effective use of octave passages.

Bars 35 and 36. The bass is used alone, doubled in octaves. This is sometimes a good way of filling in the rhythmic gap which often occurs between the end of one sentence and the beginning of another.

Last 4 bars. Another example of the effective use of octaves, the cadence formed by the two final chords providing a satisfactory finish.

Coda

Bars 26 and 27. Another device which is sometimes useful for filling in the rhythmic gap between sentences. The repeated octaves have a trumpet-like sound.

Last bar but one. Here the *tremolo* effect is in both hands.

A Note on the Organ

Since the technique of piano and organ writing is similar in many respects it may be as well to point out the fundamental differences, although a detailed description of the mechanism of the organ would require much more space than can here be afforded. It is obviously desirable that a composer should have some practical knowledge of any instrument for which he intends to write. The beginner who wishes to write for the organ is advised to consult some good book on the subject, and, if at all possible, to take a few organ lessons.

(1) Organ sound is sustained only so long as a key is held down ; if the key is raised it ceases instantly. Piano sound will continue for a time, if the sustaining pedal is held down, even though the hands are lifted from the keyboard.

(2) The piano has only one keyboard. The organ has at least two keyboards with each of which a group of pipes is linked up. These pipes are divided into sets, each set producing a different kind of tone-colour. By means of " stops " the organist is able to use any set of pipes on its own, or several sets in combination.

(3) The power of an organ note is constant however long it is sustained ; that of a piano note decreases in intensity until it dies away.

(4) The organ pedals form an additional keyboard which is played with the feet. The pedals usually take the bass notes, but it must be remembered when writing rapid passages that the feet are less agile than the hands.

(5) Organ music is written in three staves, the top and middle staves for the hands, as in piano music, and the bottom one for the feet. The usual compass of the organ is : Manuals (*i.e.* keyboards played with the hands) five octaves, starting from C on the second leger line below the bass stave ; Pedals two-and-a-half octaves starting from the same note.

It should be noted that hymn tunes intended to be played on the organ are usually written on two staves, exactly as in piano music, the organist arranging a pedal part and working out the registration (*i.e.* the selection of appropriate stops) as he goes along. The cinema organist is also in the habit of playing from ordinary piano music.

Exercises

1. Decorate the following progression in the different ways indicated.

2. Continue each of the following for a total of sixteen bars.

CHAPTER XVII

ELEMENTARY MODULATION

Music does not remain in the same key for any length of time—if it did it would soon become monotonous. A piece of music begins and ends in its principal, or " home ", key ; from time to time it wanders from this key, but however far it strays it never fails to find its way home.

The process of passing from one key to another is called **Modulation.** When music changes key temporarily, returning to its home key—or passing to yet another key—after a few chords or bars, the modulation is said to be *transient*, and is effected not by the alteration of the key-signature, but by the addition of accidentals. When the establishment of a new key is intended to be permanent (*e.g.* when one movement of a piece is followed

EXAMPLE 171

O God Our Help in Ages Past. St. Anne

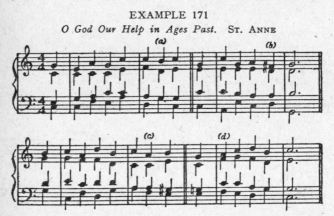

by another in a different key) and a new key-signature is adopted, the modulation is said to be *complete*.

Let us look at a simple example of transient modulation.

At (*a*) in Example 171 there is a Perfect Cadence in the key of C Major. At (*b*) there is also a Perfect Cadence, but not in the same key; the sharpened Leading Note in the first chord makes it clear that the two chords are Dominant and Tonic Triads in the key of G Major. Clearly, then, the music has wandered into that key. At (*c*) we have an Imperfect Cadence in yet another key; the G sharp in the cadence chord tells us that the music has moved into the key of A Minor. Finally at (*d*) the music finds its way back into its home key of C Major, the temporarily sharpened G being restored to its normal pitch by means of a natural.

I hope that this example will enable you to grasp the meaning of modulation; we must next consider the means.

Though music may wander from key to key it must wander purposely, not aimlessly; to modulate merely for the sake of modulation would produce vague, incoherent music. The number and nature of the modulations depend on the character of the music. Elaborate modulations which might be justified in music of great feeling and intensity would be felt to be pretentious in simple music—songs, light piano pieces, and so on—which generally needs only a few simple modulations.

In order to modulate from one key to another it is necessary to introduce some chord not in the original key (*i.e.* a chord having one or more of its notes sharpened or flattened by accidentals). This chord is known as a **modulating chord,** and without it no modulation can take place. Thus, when an Imperfect or Interrupted Cadence occurs in the Tonic key there is no modulation (although the music ends on the Dominant or Sub-dominant chord) because no modulating chord has been introduced.

The modulating chord, though clearly marking a change of key, is not in itself sufficient to establish a new key. The Dominant Seventh in Example 171 (*b*), for instance, might lead to one of several keys (*e.g.* G Major, G Minor, or E Minor}. It is clear, then, that to modulate satisfactorily at least two chords must be used to establish the new key.

Though modulation to any key is possible, the simplest and most natural modulation (which we shall consider exclusively in this chapter) occurs when the music passes from a given key to a key which is related to it. Every major or minor key has five related keys,[1] the Relative key, the key of the Dominant and its Relative, and the key of the Subdominant and its Relative.[2] Thus if we take C Major as the original key, the related keys are as follows :—

C MAJOR
A MINOR

G MAJOR   **F MAJOR**
E Minor   D Minor

Or if we take A Minor as the original key :—

A MINOR
C MAJOR

E MINOR   **D MINOR**
G Major   F Major

The keys printed in bold type are closely related to the original key ; the others are more distant relatives.

---

[1] Also called " attendant " keys.
[2] The Tonic Triads of the Related keys may be found among the Triads of the original key ; modulation between them is there-fore easily effected.

The most complete and satisfactory modulation is usually effected by the introduction of the Dominant Seventh and Tonic Chords in the new key, preceded by one or more suitable chords. The Dominant Seventh in the new key must necessarily contain a note which is foreign to the old key (*i.e.* a note which is sharpened or flattened by an accidental[1]). Thus in passing from G Major to D Major the fourth degree of the old key must be sharpened ; similarly in passing from G Major to C Major the seventh degree of the old key must be flattened.[2]

In order to modulate smoothly from one key to another it is necessary to establish some sort of connexion between the two keys. This may be effected in either of two ways.

(1) The modulation may proceed through a chord

EXAMPLE 172

---

[1] The accidentally altered note may, of course, appear in a part other than the melody, so that it cannot be assumed that the absence of accidentals in a melody means that it does not modulate ; neither can the presence of accidentals be invariably taken to indicate modulation.

[2] The fourth and seventh degrees of the scale are, in fact, the determining notes of the key. In the key of D Major, for instance, the fourth degree (G) shows that there are no more than two sharps in the key-signature, and the seventh degree (C sharp) that there are no less than two sharps.

which belongs both to the key we are in and the key to which we are going ; this is known as a **pivot chord.**[1]

Example 172 shows a modulation from C Major to G Major ; the pivot chord is marked (*a*) and the modulating chord (*b*). If the pivot chord is preceded by another chord or chords belonging to both keys (as at *a* in this example), the modulation will be smoother and more gradual.

(2) The modulation may proceed through a chord which has one or more notes belonging to both keys ; these are known as **pivot notes.**

EXAMPLE 173

Example 173 shows a modulation from C Major to F Major effected by means of a pivot note.

A series of brief transient modulations may be carried out by means of pivot notes, the Tonic Chord of

EXAMPLE 174

[1] In certain modulations the Tonic Triad of the old or the new key is the only Diatonic chord common to both keys. Thus in modulating from A Minor to D Minor, D Minor must be the pivot chord ; from A Minor to E Minor, A Minor must be the pivot chord ; and so on.

one key having a note in common with the Dominant Seventh of the next.

The Tonic Triad of the old key may generally be used with good effect to precede the Dominant Chord of the new key. Thus Example 175 shows modulations from C Major to (*a*) A Minor, (*b*) G Major, (*c*) F Major, (*d*) D Minor.

EXAMPLE 175

Example 176 shows modulations, effected by the same means, from A Minor to (*a*) C Major, (*b*) E Minor, (*c*) G Major, (*d*) D Minor, (*e*) F Major.

EXAMPLE 176

An exception to this method is the modulation from the Major Key to the Relative Minor of the Dominant Key, where it is better to precede the Dominant Chord of the new key with the Submediant or Dominant Chord of the old key[1] (*see* Examples 177 (*a*) and (*b*)).

EXAMPLE 177

All the Dominant Sevenths in Examples 176 and 177 may be preceded by some chord other than that of the Tonic of the old key (often with better effect), so long as a pivot chord or note is provided as a connecting link between the old key and the new.

When a modulation occurs in an important position (*i.e.* at the end of a phrase) the Tonic Triad in the new key may be taken in root position (as in Example 177), and the modulation made gradually by means of a pivot chord preceded by other chords common to both keys.

During the course of a phrase, or in very short sections, it is often better to use a lighter form of cadence, thus avoiding the heavy effect of a Full Close ; Example 178 shows such a modulation from C Major to (*a*) G Major, and (*b*) F Major.

---

[1] The Dominant Chord of the new key may also be preceded by the Mediant Chord of the old key (*see* Chapter XX).

EXAMPLE 178

In similar circumstances modulation by pivot note is effective ; this is much more abrupt than modulation by a pivot chord, and should never be used in an important position, as the new key will not be sufficiently established. Compare the different examples in this chapter, and notice that the more gradual modulations (such as those in Example 177) give the effect of passing *to* a key, whereas the more abrupt ones (such as those in Example 174) give the effect of passing *through* a key.

A conclusive modulation from a major key to the key of the Dominant major may often be obtained by using as a pivot chord the second inversion of the Dominant Triad in the old key ; this becomes Ic in the new key, thus forming a Cadential Six-Four.

EXAMPLE 179

The above modulation may also be taken from a minor key to the key of the Dominant minor (*e.g.* from C Minor to G Minor).

When a note in one chord is chromatically altered in the next, it should, as far as possible, be kept in the same part (*see* Examples 175 (*a*), 175 (*d*), 176 (*d*), and 177 (*b*)). Otherwise what is known as a **false relation** will result. The progression in Example 180 contains a false relation because the E natural in the first chord is in the soprano part, whereas the E flat in the second chord is transferred to the bass part. Play this progression and notice the rough effect.

EXAMPLE 180

Other false relations are not so bad, and many, such as that in Example 174, are quite unobjectionable. Only experience and aural judgment can determine whether any given progression is good or bad.

In this chapter only the mechanics of modulation have been considered. Subsequent chapters will show how these mechanics may be applied to actual composition.

Exercises

(1) Complete the following modulations by supplying two chords.

C Major to A Minor   G Minor to E♭ Major

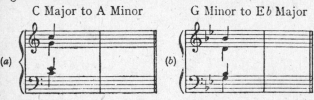

D Major to G Major   C Minor to B flat Major

(2) Write, and play on the piano, modulations to the keys given, each modulation to consist of : (1) the Tonic Triad in the old key ; (2) a pivot chord ; (3) a modulating chord ; (4) the Tonic Triad in the new key. Remember that the pivot chord must be common to both keys ; thus, in moving from C Major to G Major the pivot chord might be the Submediant or the Tonic Triad in the old key (*i.e.* the Supertonic or the Subdominant Triad in the new key).

(*a*) C Major to F Major.
(*b*) F Minor to C Minor.
(*c*) E flat Major to G Minor.
(*d*) G Major to E Minor.
(*e*) D Major to A Major.
(*f*) A Minor to F Major.
(*g*) C Minor to E flat Major.
(*h*) D Minor to A Minor.
(*i*) C Minor to F Minor.
(*j*) F Major to G Minor.
(*k*) E Minor to D Major.

(3) Write, and play on the piano, modulations to the keys given, each modulation to consist of : (1) the Tonic Triad in the old key ; (2) a modulating chord (the Dominant Seventh of the new key) containing one

or more pivot notes ; and (3) the Tonic Triad in the new key.

(*a*) C Major to A Minor.
(*b*) D Minor to C Major.
(*c*) E Minor to B Minor
(*d*) F Major to G Minor.
(*e*) A Major to E Major.
(*f*) A Minor to G Major.
(*g*) A Minor to F Major.
(*h*) B Minor to E Minor.

(4) Harmonize the following melodic fragments in four parts, modulating as directed by means of pivot chords. (*N.B.*—A note which is accidentally raised by a sharp or a natural (*e.g.* the last note but one in (*a*)) is usually, but not invariably, the new Leading Note ; similarly a note which is accidentally lowered by a flat or natural (*e.g.* the last note but one in (*d*)) is usually the new Subdominant. In either case the Dominant Seventh of the new key should be used, in root position in an inversion).

(*a*) C Major to G Major

(*b*) A Minor to G Major

(*c*) F Major to A Minor

(*d*) D Major to G Major

CHAPTER XVIII

ELEMENTARY PRINCIPLES OF FORM

If two different compositions of the same kind (*e.g.* two marches or two hymn tunes) are compared it will be found that although they differ considerably in subject-matter and detail, they have in common a certain conformity of structure which distinguishes them from other kinds of music. This is because every piece of music must be composed according to a definite plan. This plan of the music is called its Form.

Having already discussed the elementary principles underlying the construction of phrases and sentences we are now in a position to consider the composition of complete movements.[1]

Turn back to Example 171 (*O God, our Help in Ages Past*) and you will see that it may be split up into two equal sentences, which may be subdivided into two equal phrases.[2] Most simple hymn and folk tunes are composed in this form.

Now consider the first verse of this hymn.

" *O God, our help in ages past,*
Our hope for years to come,
Our shelter from the stormy blast,
And our eternal home ! "

Observe the rhyming scheme ; line one rhymes with line three, and line two with line four. Looking again at Example 171 you will see that the rhythm and

---

[1] Throughout this book " movement " is used in the sense of a complete short composition, or a complete period of a larger composition. As an example of the latter use an instrumental suite may have four movements, each complete in itself.

[2] These two-bar phrases are not divisible into sentences.

melody of each phrase corresponds to this scheme. Thus the rhythm of the first phrase is repeated in the third, and the melody of the first phrase balances, though it does not exactly imitate, that of the third. Similarly the rhythm of the second phrase is repeated in the fourth, and melodic symmetry exists between the two phrases. If we use the letters A, B, C to represent different rhymes in poetry, and different melodic and rhythmic shapes in music, we arrive at the formula A, B, A,* B,* the asterisks denoting that the phrases so marked are variations of earlier phrases, though the common pattern is clearly recognizable.

Binary and Ternary Forms

Periods which fall naturally into two equal parts are said to be in two-part or **Binary Form.** At its simplest Binary Form consists of two complete sentences (or, more rarely, phrases), the second balancing, and responding to, the first. This form, which may be expressed as A, B, is exemplified in such folk tunes as *Barbara Allen* and *The Bailiff's Daughter of Islington.* In such examples it is not unusual to find the first part ending in some related key—generally that of the Dominant, as in *Barbara Allen.* At this half-way point the effect of a Full Close in a new key is much the same as that of a Half Close in the original key. Except in hymn tunes Binary Form is seldom met with in complete movements,[1] modern ears preferring a rather more elastic form, but it is often used for periods which, though complete in themselves, occur during the course of a larger movement.

---

[1] A few complete instrumental pieces have been written in Binary Form. Brahms' Waltz in G sharp Minor, Op. 39, No. 3, and Schubert's Waltz in A flat Major, Op. 6, No. 2, each consist of two eight-bar sentences.

The form most commonly used for complete movements is the Three-Part or **Ternary Form,** which, as its name implies, consists of three divisions : (1) a musical idea, more or less self-contained ; (2) another idea, contrasting with the first, and usually in a related key ; (3) the first idea restated in the original key.

One advantage of this form is that the repetition of the first idea impresses it on the mind of the listener. In music of a popular type, which relies more on catchy melody than on development and subtlety of presentation, this repetition of the principal idea becomes almost a necessity. In simple Ternary Form the first idea is, in the majority of cases, repeated twice, the two statements together forming one-half of the complete movement. This form, which may be expressed as A, B, A, is exemplified in such folk-tunes as *The Minstrel Boy,* *The Blue Bells of Scotland,* and *The Last Rose of Summer.*[1] It will be noted from these examples that whereas in Binary Form the first part usually ends in the key in which the second part opens, in Ternary Form it closes in the Tonic Key.

The examples so far given illustrate the elementary principles underlying Two-Part and Three-Part Forms, but in practice Ternary Form is usually developed and expanded by various means which often add to its interest and value.

The Construction of Periods

We must next consider the construction of complete musical periods. With a few exceptions[2] the smallest complete period may be divided into two sentences, and

---

[1] This form is also used extensively for the Refrains, or Choruses, of many modern Dance numbers.

[2] A few complete melodies *(e.g. Barbara Allen)* consist of one sentence only, divisible into two four-bar phrases.

is therefore in simple Binary Form. In a regular period each of these sentences usually consists of two phrases. It is not essential that a modulation should be introduced during the course of a period ; in the hymn tune *Glory to Thee, My God, This Night*[1] (Tallis), for example, each sentence (and each phrase) ends with a Full Close.

For the sake of contrast, however, it is generally better to end the first sentence either with a Half Cadence in the Tonic key, or with a modulation to a related key. An example of a first sentence ending with a Half Cadence will be found in the *Old Hundredth* (*All people That on Earth do Dwell*). But it is often easier to maintain the interest and continuity of a period if a definite modulation is made, and in compositions made up of several periods insufferable monotony would soon result if every phrase began and ended in the Tonic Key.

In a period of eight-, sixteen-, or thirty-two[2] bars we cannot expect to go very far afield, and it will generally be found that one modulation to a principal key is sufficient. The most natural place for the modulation is about half-way through, the music coming to a Full Close at the end of the first half-period ; this rests the ear without giving the effect of finality, and thus prepares the way for the remainder of the period. Having established the new key the music then returns to the key of the Tonic, either direct or through other related keys. Thus Example 171 (*O God, our Help in Ages Past*) reaches the Dominant key at the half-way point, returning to the Tonic key through that of the Relative Minor. Here is another example :—

---

[1] This hymn, as well as the *Old Hundredth*, is composed of two-bar phrases.

[2] In quick waltzes and marches.

EXAMPLE 181

Danse de Fete. DELIBES

Example 181 also reaches the key of the Dominant at the half-period, returning to the Tonic key through the key of the Supertonic Minor (*i.e.* the relative of the Subdominant Major). Compare these two examples and you will find that in each the principal modulation takes place during the second phrase. In a period of four phrases it is nearly always desirable to let the music remain in the Tonic key during the first phrase.[1] Neglect of this precaution often results in such incoherent writing as the following :—

EXAMPLE 182

Because of the premature modulation in this example the original key, far from being established, is entirely lost sight of. In the majority of cases it is best to begin the modulation in the second half of the second phrase, as in the examples under consideration. During the second half-period the music may pass through several keys on its way back to the Tonic key, more modulation being possible than in the first half-period. The actual return to the old key may be delayed until the second half of the last phrase, as in Example 181.

It is important that the modulation to and from the new key should be effected gradually, that is, the old key should move to the new key through the relative chords (or relative keys) of the new key, and vice versa. Thus, although in Example 181 the modulation between the Tonic and Dominant keys begins in bar seven[2], the new key has already been suggested by the Tonic harmony in the previous bar. Similarly in moving from

---

[1] An exception to this recommendation occurs when the first phrase is divided into two sections, the second being a sequential repetition of the first (*see* Example 189).

[2] The initial half-bar is not included in the count.

the Subdominant Minor to the Tonic key, during the last three bars of this example, the return to the Tonic key is effected by means of the progression II, V7, I (the Tonic Triad of the old key becoming the Supertonic Triad of the new).

When a modulation occurs during the course of a phrase (*i.e.* when one key passes *through* another on its way to a third) care should be taken not to establish the new key too definitely. The modulation need not be effected gradually, but may be made by means of a pivot note (*e.g.* the modulation from the key of G Major to that of A Minor in Example 181). An incidental modulation may end with a Half Close, as in Example 171 (*c*), or with a Perfect Cadence with the Tonic chord in the first inversion.[1]

The next point to consider is the choice of the new key. The most usual keys to which modulation is made during the first half-period are the Dominant in a Major key and the Relative Major in a Minor key, and at first it is best to limit the principal modulation to these keys.

When experience has been gained modulation may be made to other keys, but it should be noted that a modulation to the key of the Subdominant Major, or its Relative Minor, should generally be deferred until the second half of the period, as otherwise the feeling of the original key may be weakened and the unity of the period impaired. During the second half of the period modulation to the Subdominant key may often be used with good effect to offset the previous modulation to the key of the Dominant. Thus in Example 181 the last phrase passes to the key of the Relative Minor of the Subdominant before returning to the original key.

In general, modulation to a key with a signature of

---

[1] *See also* Chapter XVII, page 161.

one sharp more (or one flat less) increases the vigour of the music, whereas the opposite procedure has the opposite effect. As far as possible, therefore, let one modulation counterbalance another.

The following modulating schemes, taken from complete periods of well-known pieces (to which reference should be made), will help to illustrate these principles.

(1) *Minuet in G* (Beethoven). 1st Period (16 bars). Key G Major.

> Phrase 1. G Major.
> Phrase 2. Through E Minor to D Major.
> Phrase 3. G Major.
> Phrase 4. G Major, C Major, A Minor, G Major.

(2) *Roses from the South* (Johann Strauss). Waltz 2, 1st Period (32 bars). Key B flat Major.

> Phrase 1. B flat Major.
> Phrase 2. To D Minor (last bar to B flat Major by pivot note).
> Phrase 3. B flat Major.
> Phrase 4. B flat Major, C Minor, B flat Major.

In each of these examples a modulation to a sharper key in one half-period is offset by a modulation to a flatter key in the other. Thus (1) proceeds from G Major (one sharp) to D Major (two sharps), and returns through C Major and A Minor (no sharps) ; (2) proceeds from B flat Major (two flats) to D Minor (one flat), and returns to C Minor (three flats).

Ternary Form

At its simplest Ternary Form consists of three periods, each complete in itself. Usually the third period is a restatement of the first, and the second a digression, though occasionally all three periods are contrasted with one another.

Simple Ternary Form is well exemplified in the *Minuet in G* of Beethoven. The first period is, in effect, a complete movement, and (as we have seen) is in Binary Form. The second period, which is called the *Trio*,[1] is also complete in itself and in Binary Form, and is well-contrasted with the first. The third period is an exact repetition of the first. Thus we have three periods, each in Binary Form, which, considered as a whole, constitute Ternary Form.

This form, which is sometimes known as **Minuet and Trio** Form, is found in such dances as the Minuet, Mazurka, and Polonaise, in the March, and in many other instrumental pieces. The Trio is usually of a more quiet and flowing character than the main section, and is frequently in another key—usually the Subdominant or the Dominant. Since these keys are so closely related to the Tonic key, it is usually possible to dispense with a modulation between the two movements.

In Minuet and Trio Form each period is generally divided into two sentences, and each sentence in the first and second periods repeated. The third period is usually played without repeats. The scheme of Beethoven's *Minuet in G* is as follows :—

1st Period :
    8-bar sentence (repeated) 8-bar sentence (repeated)
2nd Period (Trio) :
    8-bar sentence (repeated) 8-bar sentence (repeated)
3rd Period :
    8-bar sentence   8-bar sentence

In practice, instead of writing out the third period it is only necessary to add the letters D.C. (Italian *Da capo* meaning " Repeat from the beginning ") at

---

[1] Probably so-called because it was originally written in three-part harmony.

the end of the second period ; the performer will then play the first period again, leaving out the repeats according to custom.

Examples of instrumental pieces in Minuet and Trio Form are easy to find ; the following, if not already familiar, are readily accessible.

(1) *Boccaccio* March. Suppé.

(2) *Mazurka in A Minor*, Op. 68, No. 2. Chopin.

(3) *Impromptu in A flat Major*, Op. 142, No. 2. Schubert.

(4) *The Bat* (*Die Fledermaus*), Waltz No. 1. Johann Strauss.

(5) *An Important Event* (*Scenes of Childhood*). Schumann.

The three periods of which Ternary Form is made up need not be self-contained, neither is it necessary that the third period should exactly imitate the first. Greater continuity is often obtained if the first period ends in a key other than that of the Tonic ; it is then necessary to alter the final phrase of the third period so that the piece may end in the Tonic key. The second period, instead of ending with a Full Close, may lead back to the original key. Many simple piano pieces are designed on this plan, which is exemplified in the following compositions :—

(1) *Träumerei* (*Scenes of Childhood*). Schumann.

This is a superb example of a simple piano piece in Ternary Form. The first period, which is repeated, ends in the key of the Dominant. The second period, which begins in the Tonic key and modulates through several keys, is a development of the first. The third period is a repetition of the first, with the final phrase altered to bring the piece to a close in the Tonic key.

(2) *Mazurka in C Major*, Op. 7, No. 5.   Chopin.

The second period is a transposition of the first into the key of the Dominant. The third period is an exact repetition of the first.

(3) *Valse Allemande (Carnaval)*, Op. 9. Schumann.

The first period ends in the key of the Dominant, and the second begins in that key. The second phrase of the last period is considerably altered in character, in order to bring the piece to a close in the Tonic key.

The Introduction

The first period of a composition is often preceded by a preliminary phrase or movement called an **Introduction.** This varies in length from a few chords designed to summon the attention of the listener to quite a lengthy movement intended to prepare the way for the movement which is to follow.

A form of Introduction frequently found in marches and light pieces consists of a simple phrase of four or eight bars.

EXAMPLE 183
The Manhattan Beach. SOUSA

This example ends on the Dominant Triad, thus leading naturally to the first period. In a short Introduction it is not necessary that the key should be established to the same extent as in a longer period; the abrupt modulation to the Supertonic Minor key (relative to the Subdominant Major) is therefore permissible.

The Introduction must suggest the character of the music which is to follow; it would clearly be absurd to use the four bars of Example 183 to precede a dainty Gavotte or Intermezzo. Although the Introduction is structurally independent of the movement which follows, its features are frequently derived from it. Example 184 is based on the initial figure of the Dance, transposed into the Dominant key.

EXAMPLE 184

Torch Dance (Henry VIII Dances). EDWARD GERMAN
By permission of Novello & Co. Ltd.

This Introduction leads without a break into the main movement, thus maintaining the continuity of the music.

Sometimes, instead of a formal Introduction, the accompaniment may be introduced a few bars ahead of the melody, as in Example 185.[1]

---

[1] In the opening bars Schubert deliberately omits the third of the Triad to obtain a characteristically bare effect.

EXAMPLE 185

Moment Musical No. 3. Schubert

The Introductions to the waltzes of Johann Strauss and Josef Gung'l[1] are often of considerable length, though they cannot be looked upon as having any definite form. Some of them open with a slow movement in $\frac{3}{4}$, $\frac{6}{8}$, or $\frac{9}{8}$ time, or even with a march movement (Gung'l's *Immortellen* waltz begins with a Funeral March) ; this is usually followed by a second movement in waltz tempo, which leads into the waltz proper.

The Introductions to the following piano pieces[2] may be studied with advantage.

(1) *Shepherd's Dance (Henry VIII Dances)*, Edward German.

A fourteen-bar Introduction derived from subjects used in the main movement, into which it leads without a break.

(2) *Danse de Fête (Coppélia Suite)*, Leo Delibes.

A six-bar Introduction, composed of three two-bar phrases, and ending on the chord of the Dominant.

(3) *Valse des Fleurs* (*Casse-Noisette* Suite), Tschaikowsky.

A thirty-seven bar Introduction in waltz tempo, the first part of which is founded on the initial period of the main movement. This is followed by a Cadenza

---

[1] These consist of a chain of waltzes in different keys, each complete in itself, with an Introduction and a Coda.

[2] Some of these pieces were originally composed for orchestra, and subsequently transcribed for the piano.

(a free ornamental passage intended to exhibit the technical powers of the performer) based on arpeggio figures ; four bars of accompaniment then lead into the main movement.

(4) *Military March in D Major*, Op. 51, No. 1. Schubert.

A simple six-bar Introduction on Tonic harmony, which is also used, in an extended form, for the Coda.

(5) *Lied ohn Worte* in E Major, Op. 30, No. 9. Mendelssohn.

A simple two-and-a-half bar Introduction composed of arpeggio figures on Tonic harmony, followed by a Perfect Cadence.

The Coda

A tail-piece, or **Coda,** is sometimes added to the final period of a piece to make a good finish. The Coda, which may vary in length from a few chords to a lengthy movement, may be constructed either from material already used in the body of the piece, or from new material. Sometimes the Introduction (usually in a modified form) also serves as the Coda.

As its simplest the Coda is merely an extension of the Perfect Cadence with which the final period ends ; that is, a reiteration of the Tonic chord, or of the Dominant and Tonic chords. This is illustrated in Example 186.

You will see from this example that the Coda consists of a two-bar period, repeated an octave higher, plus what is virtually a one-bar period repeated four times, plus two bars reiteration of the Tonic Triad ; also that the one-bar period is a compressed version of the two-bar period. This " telescopic " form is an important

EXAMPLE 186
The Sleeping Beauty Waltz.   TSCHAIKOWSKY

characteristic of many Codas, and by its means a piece
may be brought to a smooth and gradual conclusion,
instead of being abruptly terminated. The principle is a
progressive shortening of the periods (each of which is
almost invariably repeated twice or more) followed by
an extension of the final cadence.

A perfect example of this form is found in the Coda
of Chopin's *Mazurka in C Minor*, Op. 56, No. 3. This
Coda, which is thirty-two bars long, is made up of the
following periods :—

‖: 8 bars : ‖: 4 bars : ‖: 2 bars : ‖: 1 bar : ‖: 1 bar : ‖

The so-called Codas, or Finales, to the waltzes of
Strauss, Gung'l, Waldteufel, and others, are virtually
complete movements in themselves, in which one or
more of the waltz melodies which have already been
heard are reintroduced, some new material added, and
the whole movement completed by the addition of an
Introduction and a Coda.

The following examples will repay careful study :—

(1) *Valse des Fleurs* (*Casse-Noisette* Suite). Tschaikowsky.

The last twelve bars provide another example of telescopic form. They are made up of a two-bar period (repeated twice), a one-bar period (repeated four times), and a four-bar reiteration of the final cadence.

(2) *Danse Russe Trépak* (*Casse-Noisette* Suite). Tschaikowsky.

The last sixteen bars are in telescopic form ; a four-bar period (repeated twice), a two-bar period (repeated twice), a one-bar period (repeated three times), and a final cadence bar. In order to increase the animation and excitement of this exhilarating dance, both the speed and the quantity of tone are gradually increased until the climax is reached in the last bar.

(3) *Chanson Triste.* Tschaikowsky.

The last eight bars are in telescopic form ; a two-bar period (repeated), a one-bar period (repeated), and a final two-bar period. In contrast to the previous example, the quantity of tone is decreased towards the end of this sad, contemplative movement, until it finally fades away.

(4) *Invitation to the Waltz.* Weber.

The ten-bar Coda is based on the Introduction.

The question whether an Introduction or a Coda (or both) is required in any particular piece, and, if so, what are to be the dimensions and structure, must be left to the taste and judgment of the composer. Obviously much will depend on the proportions of the piece. A simple piece consisting of two or three short periods would need only the slightest Introduction and Coda, if, indeed, it could support either ; whereas in a piece lasting several minutes quite a lengthy Introduction and Coda might not be out of place.

Marches, and dances such as the Mazurka and the Gavotte, need only a very short Introduction, and a Coda is usually unnecessary. When in doubt it is better to err on the side of brevity and simplicity—nothing is more stupid and pretentious than a long and elaborate introduction which gives place to some brief and trifling idea. It is scarcely necessary to add that neither the Introduction nor the Coda should be written until the main movement is completed, or at least roughly sketched out.

Bridge Passages

In order to secure a smooth connexion between one period and another, a short **Bridge Passage,** usually from one to four bars long, is sometimes interpolated. Such a passage is most commonly found where there is a change of key, as in the example which follows.

EXAMPLE 187

Entr'acte Gavotte (Mignon).   AMBROISE THOMAS

Four points should be noted in regard to Example 187.

(1) Since this Bridge Passage is merely a short connecting-link between two periods it is not essential that it should have any particular melodic interest, so long as it is in keeping with both periods. Sometimes such a passage may be constructed from material derived from one or both periods.

(2) The first period is in the key of C Major and the second in A Major—two keys which are not nearly-related. Such a modulation should be avoided for the time being.

(3) For the first time we meet with an example of the overlapping of two phrases. The end of the first period is actually a four-bar phrase, which is displaced by the Bridge Passage (also a four-bar phrase) before it has had time to run its course ; the last bar of the first phrase, therefore, becomes the first bar of the second. The whole melody is consequently one bar shorter than perfect symmetry would require.

Overlapping of phrases is of comparatively rare occurrence in the forms which lie within the scope of this book ; it is never *essential*, and only the composer's instinct and experience can tell him when it may be used with artistic effect.

(4) Like most Bridge Passages the one in this example is external to the form of the piece (*i.e.* it can be omitted without disturbing the form). Its sole function is to provide a smooth transition between two periods.

Other examples of Bridge Passages may be found in the following piano pieces :—

(1) *The Blue Danube.* Johann Strauss.
Waltz 1. Last three bars of second (A Major) period.

(2) *Tales from the Vienna Woods.* Johann Strauss. Waltz 3. Last four bars of second (B flat Major) period.

(3) *The Sleeping Beauty Waltz.* Tschaikowsky. Bars 105-108.

(4) *Melody in F*, Op. 3, No. 1. Rubenstein. Bars 49-56.

(5) *Washington Post March.* Sousa. Bars 59-66.

Varieties of Form

Although one or other of the simple forms already described may be used as a basis for almost any vocal or instrumental piece, many extensions and varieties of these forms are possible. In addition, there are certain instrumental pieces which cannot be said to belong either to Binary or Ternary Form.[1] Waltzes intended for dancing, for instance, often consist of four or five consecutive movements, each in Binary or Ternary form, the collection being rounded off with an Introduction and a Coda ; the form as a whole could only be described as a " set of waltzes."

It is possible to introduce any number of complete periods in a composition. But if there are four or more periods it is desirable, for the same of variety, that at least three of them be different. Thus we may have A, B, or A, B, A, but A, B, A, B, would probably be monotonous, and A, B, A, B, A, B would certainly be intolerably dull. But if a new period C (well contrasted with A and B, and probably in a different key) is introduced after A has been restated, the monotony is at once relieved, and A, or A, B, A, may then be repeated.

---

[1] A few pieces, such as the first of Bach's 48 *Preludes and Fugues*, are written in a continuous form which has virtually no division.

Many instrumental pieces are worked out according to this plan, and it may be helpful to analyse a typical example—the *Entr'acte Gavotte* from *Mignon*, by Ambroise Thomas.

Periods	Bars	Key
Introduction	4	A Major
A	‖ : 8 : ‖	A Major
B	8	E Major
Bridge Passage	4*	Modulating to A Major
A	‖ : 8 : ‖	A Major
C	8	A Major
Bridge Passage	4*	C Major
A	‖ : 8 : ‖	A Major
B	8	E Major
Bridge Passage	4*	Modulating to A Major
A	‖ : 8 : ‖	A Major
Coda	8	A Major

Ignoring the Introduction, Coda, Bridge Passages, and repeats, the form is A, B, A, C, A, B, A ; clearly an extension of simple Ternary Form. A large number of instrumental pieces have been written in this form— *e.g. The Sleeping Beauty Waltz*, and the March from the *Casse-Noisette* Suite, by Tschaikowsky. This form is sometimes shortened to A, B, A, C, A as in Schubert's *Entr'acte No.* 2 from *Rosamunde ;* it may be also found in many so-called Intermezzi and Novelty Numbers, titles which are often applied to any light piece in ⁴₄ time.

Brahms's *Hungarian Dance* No. 1 illustrates an extension of Binary Form—A, B, C, A, B—a form less frequently met with. Other varieties of form are considered in Chapter XXVI, where the characteristics of the various instrumental and vocal forms are described, the forms being arranged alphabetically for easy reference.

---

* The first bar overlaps the last bar of the previous period.

Exercises

(1) Write a waltz in simple Ternary Form, starting as follows :—

Develop this theme into a sixteen-bar period, using the following modulating scheme :—

1st section. 4 bars. As given.

2nd section. 4 bars. Sequential repetition of 1st section, with some modification at the cadence.

3rd section. 4 bars. Modulation to D Minor.

4th section. 4 bars. Cadence in Tonic key (two bars Six-Four and Dominant Chord, two bars Tonic Triad).

Add a contrasting sixteen-bar period in F Major, followed by a repetition of the first period.

(2) Write a Quick March in ₵ time on the following plan (Ternary Form).

Introduction. 4 bars. D Major.

A. 1st sentence. 16 bars. D Major, modulating to A Major during last four bars.

2nd sentence. 16 bars. To D Major (start with Dominant Seventh). *FINE.*

B. 1st sentence. 16 bars. G Major, modulating to
(TRIO)   D Major during last four bars.

2nd sentence. 16 bars. To G Major, starting with Dominant Seventh (bars 1 to 4), sequential modulation to E Minor (bars 5 to 8), modulation to G Major (bars 9 to 16), *D.C.*

(3) Develop Exercises 3 (*a*) and 3 (*b*) (Chapter XV) into complete short pieces in simple Ternary Form by adding a contrasting sentence of eight bars in the key of the Dominant, and repeating the first sentence.

CHAPTER XIX

SEQUENCES, SUSPENSIONS, AND PEDALS

Sequences

The repetition of a melodic or harmonic progression at a higher or lower pitch is known as a **Sequence.** The sequence is a most important and valuable device in composition, as a glance at almost any piece of music will show.

A sequence may be confined to a single melodic part (or a melodic part doubled in thirds or sixths), or the pattern of the original progression may be imitated in every part of the harmony. Examples of melodic sequences may be found in Example 139 (*a*) and (*b*),

EXAMPLE 188

Waltz in A flat.[1] BRAHMS

---

[1] This example also illustrates the effective use of a six-bar phrase.

and in such melodies as *The British Grenadiers* (bars 13 and 14), *John Peel* (first four bars), and Beethoven's *Minuet in G* (bars 2 and 3, and 14 and 15).

Example 188 illustrates the use of the harmonic sequence.

Notice that the intervals in the first progression are exactly repeated in the second (the bass is taken down an octave to avoid a repetition of the previous note). This is called a **Real Sequence.**

More often than not, however, the intervals in the first progression are not always repeated exactly ; a **Tonal Sequence** is then formed.

EXAMPLE 189

Mazurka in G Minor. CHOPIN

You will see that the intervals of the first progression are not exactly preserved in the repetition (*e.g.* the first progression ends with a minor chord, and the repetition with a major). A tonal sequence is generally smoother in effect, and easier to handle, than a real one. Another example of a tonal sequence will be found on page 191, Example 199.

The sequences in Examples 188 and 189 are modulatory. As the effect of these modulations is only transient, one counter-balancing the other, a modulatory sequence may be, and often is, used at the beginning of a period. Many of Chopin's *Mazurkas* open in this way.

A progression may be imitated at any interval above

or below, but in practice the limit of a third is rarely exceeded.

The number of repetitions should not exceed two, or three at the most, otherwise the procedure becomes mechanical and monotonous. The final repetition should form a satisfactory finish to the passage.

In four-part writing certain rules are relaxed in regard to tonal sequences, especially those which are non-modulatory (*i.e.* which do not leave the key). The Leading Note may be doubled, and may either rise or fall ; and augmented intervals may occur in the voice parts. These relaxations apply only to the *repetitions* of the original progression, and not to the progression itself.

The following additional examples illustrate the use of the harmonic sequence.

(1) *Mazurka in F sharp Minor*, Op. 6, No. 1. Chopin.

This opens with a two-bar sequence (one repetition a minor third higher), followed by a one-bar sequence (three repetitions a tone lower). Both sequences are tonal and modulatory.

(2) *Mazurka in F Major*, Op. 68, No. 3. Chopin.

This opens with a two-bar tonal sequence, with two repetitions a minor third lower. The first repetition modulates to the key of the Mediant Minor (relative to the Dominant Major), and the second returns to the Tonic key.

(3) *Impatience.* Song. Schubert.

The first four bars of the verse provide a good illustration of the effective use of the tonal sequence (one repetition a tone higher). Both the original progression and the repetition are modulatory, the former passing to the key of the Supertonic Minor, and the latter to the Mediant Major (not a closely-related key). Notice that the harmonic plan in the repetition is slightly altered, the third chord being in the first inversion instead of in root position.

(4) *Military March in D Major*, Op. 51, No. 1. Schubert.

Bars 32–39 illustrate the repetition of a four-bar phrase a tone lower, thus forming a tonal sequence.

Suspensions

In proceeding from one chord to another, a note which would normally descend or ascend to the next note of the scale is sometimes held back until the other notes have been sounded. This note is called a **Suspension.** If the note is part of the new chord no special treatment is necessary ; if it is not it becomes what is known as a prepared discord, and must be resolved upon the note it has suspended.

EXAMPLE 190

You will see from Example 190 that a suspension may be resolved upwards or downwards. In either case it must move by step to the next note of the scale. Where the step is a tone resolution upwards is generally the more effective ; where it is a semitone either resolution is often good. It is not essential that the suspended note should be tied to the previous note, as in Example 190 ; it is often better to sound it a second time, as in the example which follows.

EXAMPLE 191

Lied ohn Werte in A Major.   MENDELSSOHN

A suspension may appear in any part, including the bass. It may sometimes be doubled in thirds or sixths, as in Example 192 (*a*), but this doubling needs care and should be used sparingly at present. An excellent effect is often produced by suspending the three upper notes (in four-part harmony) of the Dominant Seventh at a Perfect Cadence, as in Example 192 (*b*).

EXAMPLE 192

The following points should be carefully noted.

(1) A suspension must be prepared ; that is, the discord must be in the same part in the preceding chord. If the discords in Example 192 (*a*) and 192 (*b*) were unprepared they would cease to be suspensions and become accented passing notes.

(2) The discord should not occur on a weaker part of the bar than its resolution.

EXAMPLE 193

Bad.

Compare the effect of the above progression with that of Example 190 (*a*).

(3) The note on which the discord is about to resolve should not usually be doubled in the upper parts.

EXAMPLE 194

Bad.

Play the above progression and you will feel the harsh effect caused by the clash of the discord with the note of resolution.

When the note of resolution is doubled in the bass, however, as in Example 190 (*b*), the effect is quite satisfactory.

When the suspension occurs in the bass, the note of resolution should not be sounded in an upper part.

(4) A suspension may be resolved on any chord; the chord of resolution at (*a*) in Example 191 is the third inversion of the Dominant Seventh, and at (*b*) the first inversion of the same chord.

(5) A bad progression is not made good by the introduction of a suspension.

EXAMPLE 195

In the example above the objectionable effect of consecutive octaves between the extreme parts is not mitigated by the suspension.

(6) The most useful and satisfactory suspensions for general use are the following :—

(*a*) The suspended 9th (Example 190 (*a*)). The suspended note is a 9th above the root of the chord, and resolves downwards by step.

(*b*) The suspended 4th (Example 192 (*b*), alto voice). The suspended note is a 4th above the root of the chord, and resolves downwards by step.

(*c*) The suspended 6th (Example 191 (*a*)). The suspended note is a 6th above the root of the chord, and resolves downwards by step.

(*d*) The suspended 7th (Example 190 (*b*)). The suspended note is a 7th above the root of the chord, and resolves *upwards* by step.

Of these suspensions the first two are the most common.

Ornamental Resolution of Suspensions

A suspension is sometimes resolved ornamentally.

(*a*) By moving by leap or step to another note of the chord of resolution before being resolved (Example 196 (*a*)).

(*b*) By leaping to a passing note a step above or below the note of resolution (Example 196 (*b*) and (*c*)).

EXAMPLE 196

Suspensions often provide a means of keeping the music flowing, especially at intermediate cadences, as in Example 191 (*a*) and (*b*).

Pedals

A **Pedal**, or **Pedal-Note**, is a note (usually in the bass) which is sustained through a succession of chords of which it may or may not form an essential part.[1]

EXAMPLE 197

In Example 197 the Pedal does not form a part of the second, sixth, and eighth chords.

The most usual notes for a Pedal (and the only ones which should be used at present) are the Dominant and the Tonic. An example of a Dominant Pedal (doubled in octaves) is shown in Example 198, and one of a Tonic Pedal in Example 197.

---

[1] One of the simplest Pedals is the drone-bass of the bagpipes.

EXAMPLE 198

A Dominant Pedal, in the words of Sir Alexander Macfarren[1] (1813–1887), "produces the effect of climax, leading us from chord to chord more and more to desire, more and more to expect the close to which it must lead." A Tonic Pedal " has the effect of confirming the conclusion indicated by a Perfect Cadence, and expresses satisfaction or rest."

Sometimes the Tonic and Dominant Pedals are sounded at the same time, as in Example 199; this forms what is known as a Double Pedal.

EXAMPLE 199

Shepherd's Dance (Henry VIII Dances). EDWARD GERMAN
By permission of Novello & Co. Ltd.

---

[1] *Six Lectures in Harmony.*

Bass Pedals

The following points should be carefully noted :—

(1) The Pedal should form part of the first and last chords over (or under) it. This point is exemplified in the three examples already quoted.

(2) When the Pedal does not form an essential part of the harmony, the part next above it should be regarded as the real bass, and should conform to the rules for the progression of a bass part.

(3) When Tonic and Dominant Pedals occur in succession the Dominant is usually preceded by the Tonic.

(4) Modulations may occur on a Bass Pedal. These are by no means easy to handle, and the beginner is advised not to attempt to modulate until he has learned to handle non-modulatory Pedals with comfort.

The most usual modulations are :—

(*a*) On a Dominant Pedal.

Major Key.	Supertonic Minor.
	Mediant Minor.
Minor Key.	Subdominant Minor.

(*b*) On a Tonic Pedal.

Major Key.	Subdominant Major or Minor.
Minor Key.	Subdominant Minor.

Sometimes a Bass Pedal is doubled in an upper part, in which case the recommendations already outlined apply without exception.

EXAMPLE 200

Inverted Pedals

A Pedal is sometimes sustained in an upper part instead of in the bass ; it is then said to be inverted.

EXAMPLE 201

It is generally best to limit the harmony beneath an Inverted Pedal to some simple progression, such as a succession of Triads in their first inversions, as in Example 201. It is better not to sound the Dominant Chord below a Tonic Pedal—the effect is invariably ugly.

You will notice that the second bar of Example 201 is a sequential repetition of the first, modulating to the key of the Dominant. In order to preserve the pattern of the original progression, the Leading Note in the fourth chord falls to the fifth of the next chord.

Practical Use of Pedals

A short Tonic Pedal may be used at the beginning or the end of a movement or period, especially when a tranquil effect is wanted (*e.g.* in pastoral movements and in cradle songs). It is particularly useful as an extension of the last phrase of a melody, or as a short Coda. Example 200 could be used in this way ; it will be seen that this passage is, in effect, a Plagal extension of a Perfect Cadence.

The Dominant Pedal may sometimes be used with good effect in a Bridge Passage ; the Inverted Pedal in

Example 201 might well form a link between a period in the Tonic key and another in the Subdominant key. The Dominant Pedal may also be used to precede a final close, especially when working up to a climax.

Both the Tonic and the Dominant Pedals may, of course, be used during the course of a movement ; the uses outlined are merely those which are of most value to the beginner.

In instrumental music a Pedal is sometimes ornamented by means of auxiliary notes, or given some rhythmic form.

EXAMPLE 202

Example 202 (*a*) and (*b*) may be used to decorate a Bass Pedal and (*c*) an Inverted Pedal. Other forms of decoration are possible ; the Inverted Pedal in Example 201, for instance, is decorated by means of a trill.

Examples of the use of the Pedal are shown in Examples 185 and 236. Other examples may be found in the works of Tschaikowsky, Sir Edward German, Sir Arthur Sullivan, and others. Here are a few taken from well-known compositions.

(1) *Danse Arabe* (*Casse-Noisette* Suite). Tschaikowsky.

Here a Double Pedal alternating with the octave of the Tonic forms a rhythmic pattern which is used throughout the movement, except for a few bars in which the Tonic Pedal appears by itself.

(2) *Danse Russe Trepak* (*Casse-Noisette* Suite). Tschaikowsky.

The Tonic Pedal is used extensively during the first period (bar 2, bars 5 to 8, and so on), and in the first part of the Coda; eight bars from the end it gives way to a Double Pedal. Observe that the Pedal is not sustained, but is sounded on the second half of each beat. It is not, of course, necessary that a Pedal should be sounded continuously; it is often less ponderous in the form of a rhythmic figure, with rests intervening.

(3) *When a Merry Maiden Marries* (*The Gondoliers*). Sullivan.

Bars 1 to 7 of this song illustrate the effective use of a Double Pedal under Tonic and Dominant harmony. In bars 11 to 14 a Triple Pedal is formed by the Tonic, Dominant, and octave of the Tonic. Sir Arthur Sullivan made liberal use of Pedals throughout this song and the Chorus which precedes it.

(4) *Roses from the South.* Johann Strauss.

A Double Pedal is used in bars 1 to 6, and a Dominant Pedal, in *tremolo* octaves, in bars 24 to 31 of the Introduction. The four bars preceding Waltz 1 illustrate the use of an Inverted Pedal in a Bridge Passage.

(5) *Wiegenlied.* Brahms.

The accompaniment of this cradle song is based on the Tonic Pedal throughout.

Exercises

(1) Re-write Examples 190, 191, 192, and 196, removing all suspensions.

(2) Harmonize the following melodic fragments, introducing suspensions at each*.

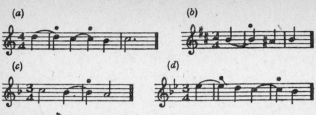

(3) Add parts alto and tenor.

(4) Add parts for alto, tenor, and bass.

(5) Develop the following phrase into a sixteen-bar period for piano, introducing Pedals where appropriate.

CHAPTER XX

MORE SECONDARY TRIADS

The two Secondary Triads which remain to be considered occur on the third and the seventh degrees of the scale.

In major keys the Mediant Triad is minor; in minor keys it is augmented. We shall consider the treatment of each separately.

The Mediant Triad in Major Keys

The introduction of the Mediant Triad in a major key requires a good deal of discrimination, and for the present it should be used in root position only when it is preceded and followed by chords with which it has one or two notes in common; *i.e.* I, V, VI, VII, and V7. The most useful progression is from IIIa to VIa.

EXAMPLE 203

In the first inversion the Mediant Triad should be preceded and followed by (*a*) a first inversion a step away, or (*b*) by chords with which it has one or two notes in common.

EXAMPLE 204

Either the root or the third may be freely doubled; the fifth, being the Leading Note, should not normally be doubled.

The Mediant Triad in Minor Keys

In minor keys the Mediant Triad is a discord requiring special treatment. The most satisfactory progression is from III to VI.

EXAMPLE 205

When the Mediant Triad is used in root position the best note to double is the root; in the first inversion either the root or the third may be doubled. The fifth, being the Leading Note, should not be doubled, and should resolve upwards by step. In root position it is generally best to prepare the discordant note (*i.e.* the augmented fifth) by sounding it in the same voice in the previous chord (as in Example 205 (*a*)).

The Triad on the Leading Note

This Triad is diminished in both major and minor keys. For practical purposes it is only used in its first inversion, the root position being unsatisfactory on account of the diminished fifth.

In its first inversion the Triad on the Leading Note may often be used with good effect in places where Dominant harmony would otherwise be satisfactory.

EXAMPLE 206

You will see from Example 206 that VIIb is actually an incomplete second inversion of the Dominant Seventh. It is generally best to double the third of the chord ; the root, being the Leading Note, should not be doubled.

VIIb is best followed by Ia, Ib, or VIa. It should not be followed by Va, though Va may precede VIIb if the first chord occurs on a stronger beat than the second.

The Melodic Minor Scale

Although the notes of the Harmonic Minor Scale are used in the construction of the principal chords in the minor key, it is possible to use the sharpened sixth of the Melodic Minor Scale in ascending, and the flattened seventh in descending, thus avoiding the interval of the augmented second.[1]

If you will refer back to the table of Triads formed on the seven degrees of the Harmonic Minor Scale (Ex-

---

[1] The use of the Melodic Minor Scale in connexion with passing notes has already been discussed in Chapter XV.

ample 117, page 101) you will see that the sixth degree of
the scale is found in Triads II, IV, and VI, and the
seventh degree in Triads III, V, and VII. If the sixth
degree is sharpened, and the seventh degree flattened,
the following Triads will be formed.

EXAMPLE 207
KEY OF C MINOR
Ascending　　　　Descending

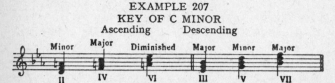

For the present these chords should only be used
when a melodic part proceeds scale-wise; that is,
upwards from the Dominant to the Leading Note, or
downwards from the Tonic to the Submediant, as in
Example 208.

EXAMPLE 208

The six progressions in Example 208 illustrate :—

(a) The sharpened sixth treated as the 5th of the Minor Triad on II.

(b) The flattened seventh treated as the 5th of the Major Triad on III.

(c) The sharpened sixth treated as the 3rd of the Major Triad on IV.

(d) The flattened sixth treated as the 3rd of the Minor Triad on IV. This Triad is best in the first inversion.

(e) The sharpened sixth treated as the root of the Diminished Triad on VI. This Triad is unsatisfactory in root position, and should be used only in the first inversion. When followed by VIIb (also a Diminished Triad) the effect is usually best when the passage is taken in three-part harmony.

(f) The flattened seventh treated as the root of the Major Triad on VII. This Triad is best in the first inversion.

The following points should be noted.

(1) The sharpened sixth should not be doubled ; the flattened seventh may be doubled.

(2) When the flattened seventh is used the next chord but one should contain the Leading Note ; otherwise the tonalty of the music tends to become indefinite.

The False Relation which occurs (e.g. in Example 208 (b), (d), and (f), between B flat in the second chord and B natural in the fourth) is unobjectionable.

(3) The two forms of Minor Scale should not be mixed (e.g. in the key of C Minor the notes A flat and A natural, or B flat and B natural, should not occur in consecutive chords).

Melodic passages containing the sharpened sixth, or the flattened seventh, may often be harmonized more simply and effectively by means of a short Pedal on the Dominant, as in Example 209 (*a*), or an accented passing note, as in Example 209 (*b*).

EXAMPLE 209

Exercises

(1) Write (and play) the following progressions in four-part harmony, in the keys indicated.

(*a*)	C Major.	Ia	Va	IIIa	Ia
(*b*)	A Minor.	Ia	Va	IIIa	VIa
(*c*)	E flat Major.	Ib	IIIb	V7c	Ib
(*d*)	C Minor.	IIb	Va	IIIa	VIa
(*e*)	D Major.	Ib	IVa	VIIb	VIa
(*f*)	D Minor.	Ia	VIIb	Ib	
(*g*)	E Minor.	Va	IIa	Va	Ia
(*h*)	F Minor	Ib	VIIb	VIb	Vb

(2) Add parts for alto, tenor, and bass, introducing at least one Mediant Triad and one Leading Note Triad in each exercise.

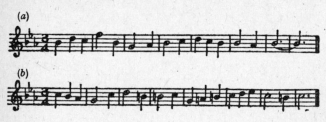

(3) Add parts for soprano, alto, and tenor, introducing Secondary Triads where appropriate.

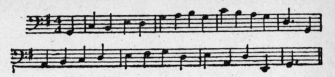

CHAPTER XXI

IRREGULAR PHRASE CONSTRUCTION

Again comparing the construction of poetry and music let us consider this verse :[1]

> " Swiftly walk o'er the western wave,
>   Spirit of Night !
> Out of the misty eastern cave—
> Where, all the long and lone daylight,
> Thou wovest dreams of joy and fear
> Which make thee terrible and dear—
>   Swift be thy flight ! "

Although these lines vary in length, the balance and proportion of the verse is quite satisfactory.

In compositions other than dance music and marches we frequently find a similar departure from normal four- or eight-bar phrases. Complete uniformity in phrase length invariably presents a certain squareness and rigidity of form, and though in short pieces this may not result in monotony, in longer pieces some variety is usually an artistic necessity.

In this chapter we shall consider some of the different ways in which a period may be modified by the extension or contraction of a phrase.

(1) The simplest method of extending a period is by repeating or delaying the final cadence.

Example 210 shows how an ordinary four-bar phrase may be extended to six bars by repeating the last

---

[1] *To the Night.*   Shelley.

EXAMPLE 210

section ; the extension will at once be apparent if the example is played first as written, and then leaving out the two bars enclosed by the square bracket.

You will see that the extension in Example 210 is made by introducing an Interrupted Cadence (V^7, VI) at the (normal) end of the period, so that a Full Close is then required to bring it to a satisfactory conclusion. By this means the flow of the music is uninterrupted.

Occasionally Ib may be substituted for VI, thus forming an Inverted Cadence ; in other cases the final Full Close instead of being delayed may be repeated (often in a modified form) or the final chord reiterated so as to strengthen the conclusive effect of the cadence, and to form a kind of miniature Coda to the period.

Examples of extension by cadential repetition or delay may be found in the following pieces :—

(a) *O, Canada* !   C. Lavallée.
Four-bar extension at end of Chorus.
(b) *Lied ohn Werte*.   Mendelssohn.
Op. 19, No. 6.   Bars 12 to 17.
Op. 53, No. 20.   Bars 13 to 5 from the end.

(2) Another method of extension is the interpolation of one or more bars during the course of a phrase. This interpolation may take the form of (a) the more or less exact repetition of a bar, or bars, at the same pitch or at a higher one ; (b) the repetition of some melodic figure or

phrase by sequence; (c) the introduction of one or more entirely new bars, interrupting the normal flow of the phrase.

An example of an exact repetition is given below.

EXAMPLE 211

Serenade. SCHUBERT

In this example the second half of a four-bar phrase is repeated at a higher pitch as a sort of echo.[1]   This device should be used sparingly, for if every cadence is echoed the periods soon become almost as square and monotonous as a succession of four-bar phrases.

Next we have an example of sequential repetition.

EXAMPLE 212

Duet from Faust. GOUNOD

Here a four-bar phrase is followed by another phrase of five bars; but if the extension is omitted the second phrase is then reduced to normal four-bar rhythm. Another example of extension by sequential repetition

---

[1] An effective use of this effect is found in *Iolanthe* (Sir Arthur Sullivan); in No. 3 (Entrance of Strephon) a figure of six notes is first sung, and then echoed by the shepherd's pipe.

may be found in the *Flower Song* from the same opera. Sequential repetition generally occurs on the fifth and sixth bars of an eight-bar sentence (as in Example 212), but it may occur on other bars.

The introduction of entirely new bars in a phrase is less commonly met with. A familiar example is Dibdin's sea song *Tom Bowling*, in which two new bars (the last but two) are interpolated, thus making a six-bar phrase.

(3) A third method of extension is the augmentation of a cadence by doubling, or otherwise increasing, the length of the notes.

EXAMPLE 213

The Sentry's Song (Iolanthe).   SULLIVAN
By permission of Chappell & Co. Ltd.

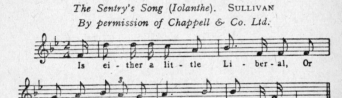

In Example 213 it is evident that the cadence notes are doubled in length, thus extending the phrase to five bars. When cadential augmentation is used it generally, though not invariably, occurs during the last phrase of a period. Sometimes, as in Example 213, it is used to give greater weight and importance to the last few notes of a song.

(4) Contraction of a phrase is less frequently met with than extension, and is more difficult to handle. We have already come across an example of the overlapping of two phrases (Example 187, page 177), the end

of one phrase coinciding with the beginning of another. A common example of this overlapping occurs in the form of the Anglican chant. Reference to any single (or double) chant will show that it consists of two (or four) phrases, the first (and third) containing three bars, and the second (and fourth) four bars. In these chants the notes which do double duty as the close of one phrase and the opening of the next, are always " reciting notes " of indefinite length ; the form is therefore well adapted to its purpose.

Except in the composition of chants, which follow a set form, the beginner is advised to leave phrase contraction alone until he has mastered the construction of regular phrases.

The devices of phrase extension are easier to handle ; the main difficulty is knowing *when* to use them. In this, as in all matters of artistic effect, the composer must ultimately be guided by his feeling and taste. In the early stages, however, careful analysis of the works of other composers will provide him with suitable models for imitation.

Phrases of Two, Three, and Six Bars

Two-bar phrases are occasionally met with. *God Save The Queen* has already been cited as an example of two-bar rhythm, and it is also a remarkably good instance of an irregular melody. The two sentences into which it is divided are of unequal length, the first consisting of three phrases of two bars each, and the second of four phrases of two bars each.

Three- and six-bar phrases are of very rare occurrence ; it may, however, be worth while to give an example of each.

Three-bar phrase: *There was a time* from *The Gondoliers* (Sullivan), No. 5, bars 3 to 8.

Six-bar phrase: *Liebestraum* (Liszt), bars 1 to 12.

Exercises

(1) Take several regular eight-bar sentences, such as Example 92, and extend them (*a*) an extra two bars, and (*b*) an extra four bars, by delaying the final cadence.

(2) By reference to different compositions find examples of (*a*) extension by interpolation during the course of a phrase, and (*b*) extension by augmentation of a cadence. Write out the phrases as they would appear with the extension omitted.

CHAPTER XXII

SECONDARY SEVENTHS

We have seen that by adding to the Dominant Triad a note a seventh above the root, the chord of the Dominant Seventh may be formed. In the same way chords of the Seventh may be formed on the other degrees of the Major or Minor Scale; these chords are called **Secondary Sevenths.**

EXAMPLE 214

KEY OF C MAJOR

Play the first phrase of Example 171 (*O God, Our Help in Ages Past*), listening carefully to the sixth chord. Compare this chord with the table above, and you will see that it is a Secondary Seventh on the Supertonic. Like all Secondary Sevenths it is a dissonant chord, and its introduction gives a rich and pleasing flavour to the harmony.

EXAMPLE 215

The Secondary Seventh most frequently used is the one on the Supertonic, which provides a useful approach to the Perfect, Interrupted, or Imperfect Cadence.

Secondary Sevenths should be resolved according to the following rules :—

(1) The seventh should be prepared (*i.e.* it should appear in the preceding chord in the same voice).

(2) The seventh should fall a step.

(3) The bass should rise either a step or a fourth, or fall a fifth.

These rules are freely broken by modern composers but should be strictly observed by the beginner.

A Secondary Seventh may be resolved upon another Secondary Seventh (or upon the Dominant Seventh), the third of one chord remaining to become the seventh of the next. In this way a sequence of sevenths may be produced. Such a sequence is more common in a major key than in a minor.

EXAMPLE 216

When a sequence of Secondary Sevenths in root position is written in four-part harmony it is necessary to omit the fifth of every alternate chord and double the root ; the Leading Note may be doubled in these circumstances. This progression, like all sequences, should be used with discretion as it has become something of a cliché ; this warning is all the more necessary because the beginner, whose experience and taste is only partially formed, is usually attracted towards such progressions, and is apt to flog them to death.

A Secondary Seventh, like the Dominant Seventh, has three inversions; the second and third inversions are of no great value to the beginner and are not considered in this chapter. The first inversion is useful, and presents no special difficulties.

The Secondary Seventh on the Supertonic, in its first inversion, resembles the Subdominant Triad with the sixth added to it, and for this reason is called the chord of the **Added Sixth.** It is particularly useful as a substitute for the Subdominant Triad. It may be resolved on the chord of the Dominant, as in Example 215 (c), or on the Tonic Triad or Cadential Six-Four, as in the example below.

EXAMPLE 217

The Secondary Seventh on the Submediant may be resolved on the Dominant Triad, or Dominant Seventh.

EXAMPLE 218

The Secondary Seventh on the Leading Note may be resolved on the Tonic Triad.

EXAMPLE 219

VII7 is most useful in the first inversion, and is usually preceded by IVa, as in the above examples. This chord may also be used in brief transient modulations, to replace, or precede, the Dominant Seventh (*i.e.* the modulating chord).

EXAMPLE 220

Secondary Sevenths in the Minor Key

The only Secondary Sevenths in the minor key which are of practical use to the beginner are those on the Supertonic, the Submediant, and the Leading Note. Examples of two of these progressions have already been given (Example 215 (c) and Example 219 (b)). The sharpened sixth and the flattened seventh of the Melodic Minor Scale may be used when required, so long as the conditions outlined in Chapter XX are fulfilled. Example 221 illustrates the use of these intervals.

EXAMPLE 221

Exercises

(1) Write (and play) the following progressions in four-part harmony, in the keys indicated:

(a) C Major.	IVa	II7a	Va	Ia
(b) D Minor.	Ib	II7a	Va	Ia
(c) D Major.	Ib	II7b	Va	Ia
(d) A Minor.	Va	VI7a	V7b	Ia
(e) E flat Major.	Ib	II7b	V7a	Ia
(f) E Minor.	IVa	VIIb	Ib	Ia

(2) Continue the following sequences downwards, bringing each passage to a suitable conclusion after a few repetitions.

(3) Add parts for alto, tenor and bass, introducing Secondary Sevenths where appropriate.

CHAPTER XXIII

THE CHORD OF THE DOMINANT NINTH

By adding to the Dominant Seventh a major or minor ninth from the root, the chord of the **Dominant Ninth** may be formed.

EXAMPLE 222

Play Example 222, and you will probably agree that the Dominant Ninth, with its added dissonance, is far more striking than the Dominant Seventh ; the major and minor forms differ in effect, but both have in common a certain poignant quality.

The Dominant Ninth contains five different notes, and there are, therefore, four possible inversions. In four-part harmony one note must be omitted ; generally the fifth in root position, and the root in inversions.

The Dominant Ninth may be resolved in two different ways : (1) on the Dominant Seventh, in which case the ninth may be regarded as an unessential note (an accented passing note or a suspension), or (2) on a chord other than that of the Dominant Seventh, in which case the ninth is an essential note. We shall consider each resolution separately.

The Ninth as an Unessential Note

The resolution of the ninth on the Dominant Seventh does not require any special consideration, the ninth being treated like any other unessential note. An example of this resolution will be found at (c) in Example 141. The following points should be noted, however :—

(1) The ninth may either fall to the root of the Dominant Seventh, or rise to the third. When it falls the root may be doubled in the bass, but not in any other part. When it rises the third should not be doubled in any part.

(2) In the major key either the major or the minor ninth may be used as an unessential note. In the minor key the minor ninth must fall to the root of the Dominant Seventh, as in Example 219 (b) ; if it were to rise to the third, the interval of an augmented second would be formed.[1] The major ninth (*i.e.* the sharpened sixth of the Melodic Minor Scale) is used when the melody proceeds upwards from the Dominant to the Leading Note, as in Example 223 (b).

EXAMPLE 223

Example 223 (a) illustrates a useful progression (which may also be used in the major key) ; here both

---

[1] The interval of an augmented second is occasionally used in instrumental music when some special effect is wanted (*e.g.* a melody principally composed of augmented seconds has a decided Eastern flavour).

the A flat in the first chord and the E flat in the second
are treated as passing notes.

(3) The ninth may sometimes resolve by falling a
seventh to the third of the Dominant Seventh.

EXAMPLE 224

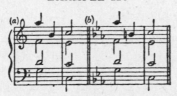

In these circumstances the gap of a ninth between
the two highest parts is justifiable.

(4) The Dominant Seventh must be resolved in the
usual way.

The Ninth as an Essential Note

When the ninth is an essential note the Dominant
Ninth usually resolves on the Tonic Triad.   Normally
the major ninth is used in a major key (Example 224 (*a*))
and the minor ninth in a minor key (Example 224 (*b*)) ;
the minor ninth may, however, be used in a major key,

EXAMPLE 225

when it becomes a *chromatic* chord (*i.e.* a chord containing one or more notes which though foreign to the Diatonic Scale do not produce modulation).

The Dominant Ninth may also resolve on the Secondary Seventh on the Submediant, the Secondary Seventh then resolving on a Dominant Seventh, as in Example 255.

The most usual position of the Dominant Ninth is with the ninth in the top part, falling to the fifth of the Tonic Triad (Example 222 (*a*) and (*b*)). Other resolutions are of little value to the beginner.

Since the root of the Dominant Ninth is usually omitted in the inversions, these chords are identical with the Secondary Sevenths formed on the Leading Note of the Major and Minor Scales. The treatment of these chords has already been considered in Chapter XXII. The inversions of the Dominant *Minor* Ninth (with the root omitted) are generally described as chords of the **Diminished Seventh**; they may be used in both major and minor keys, being chromatic chords in the former.

Exercises

(1) Write (and play) the following progressions in four-part harmony, in the keys indicated :

(*a*) G Major.	IIa	V9a	V7a	I	
(*b*) C Minor.	Ia	V9a	V7a	Ia	
(*c*) C Major.	Ia	V9a	VI7a	V7b	Ia
(*d*) F Minor.	Ia	V9	VI7a	V7b	Ia

(2) Add alto, tenor, and bass parts to the following, introducing the Dominant Ninth where appropriate.

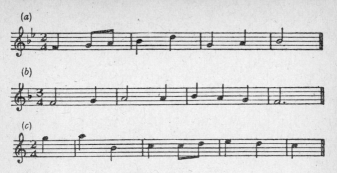

Suggestions for further study

With the chord of the Dominant Ninth we come to the end of the harmonic resources of this book. No attempt has been made to deal with the chords of the Dominant Eleventh and Thirteenth, Chromatic Harmony, and modulation to unrelated keys ; it would be impossible to give these subjects adequate treatment in a book of this size. When these chapters have been mastered advanced harmony may be studied in such books as *Elementary Harmony*, Part 3 (Kitson), or *Melody and Harmony*, Part 3 (Macpherson). At this stage the study of elementary counterpoint (the art of combining melodies) may be begun, and continued *pari passu* with that of harmony. *Introduction to Counterpoint* (R. O. Morris) or *Melody and Harmony*, Book I, may be recommended.

Meanwhile the beginner has ample material with which to compose simple pieces of his own, and I would urge him not to go further until he has learned to use the resources treated of in this book with ease and assurance. Only if the foundations are well and truly laid can he hope to build his ideas into a sound musical structure.

CHAPTER XXIV

·THE TREATMENT OF VOCAL MUSIC

Classification of Voices

Voices are classified according to their compass and vocal quality. The compass of the four main divisions—Soprano, Contralto, Tenor, and Bass—has already been given in Chapter III. There are also two subdivisions—Mezzo-Soprano, and Baritone.

Soprano. The highest of all voices. It is divided into three classes:—

(*a*) Dramatic Soprano, a powerful and emotional voice.

(*b*) Lyric Soprano, the most usual form of soprano voice, light and agile.

(*c*) Coloratura Soprano, a voice with a bright, flute-like quality, a high range, and an ability to sing rapid passages.

Mezzo-Soprano. The commonest of female voices, midway between the soprano and contralto. The compass is about a third lower than that of a soprano; the tone is full and flexible.

Contralto. The true contralto voice is rare; it has a rich, expressive quality, but is less flexible than the higher voices.

Tenor. The highest male voice. It is divided into two classes:—

(*a*) Light (or Lyric) Tenor, the male counterpart of the Lyric Soprano. A brilliant, flexible voice.

(*b*) Heavy (or Robust) Tenor, a full, vigorous voice corresponding to the Dramatic Soprano.

The lower notes of the average tenor voice are usually poor and weak, compared with those of a baritone.

Baritone. The commonest of male voices, midway between the tenor and the bass. The tone is lighter and more flexible than that of the bass; the compass about a third lower than that of the tenor.

Bass. The deepest male voice. It is divided into two classes:—

(*a*) Basso Cantante (or Lyric Bass), sometimes called Bass-Baritone; it has qualities similar to those of the other lyric voices.

(*b*) Basso Profundo (or Deep Bass), the most powerful of all voices, with the lowest range.

The lowest notes of any voice are the weakest, and the highest the most powerful. The notes which lie in between constitute the normal range, or *tessitura*, of the voice, and the main part of a vocal composition should be written within this compass. The extreme notes should be used with moderation and judgment; they are far more striking in effect, and much less fatiguing to sing, if the previous passages have been confined to the middle part of the compass.

In writing high notes the vowel sounds on which they are to be sung must be taken into consideration; closed vowels, such as " ee " are much more difficult to produce than open ones, such as " ah ". The composer who does not sing himself will do well to study some good treatise on singing. Much useful information may be found in Mr. Plunket Greene's *Interpretation in Song* (Macmillan).

Setting Words to Music

Many amateur composers seem to have little or no idea how words should be set to music. As to the first step—the selection of a suitable poem—it is difficult to give any useful advice. It is obvious that the composer should choose a poem which is well written and which appeals to him ; he cannot be expected to put his heart into the setting of some piece of doggerel which he dislikes. Many of the non-copyright verses have already been set to music (some many times), and it is doubtful whether there is room for further settings of such poems as *Gather ye Rosebuds*, or *Orpheus with his Lute*. But a search through any anthology of English verse will reveal many lesser-known poems of which free use may be made. There are some good modern verses which have not been used, but as these are copyright the permission of the author should be obtained before the setting is begun.

The lyric having been chosen, it should be read aloud several times, and the sentiment, accentuation, and inflexion of the words carefully noted. It is obvious that lively words should not be set to slow music, and vice versa. What is perhaps less obvious is that the accented syllables of the verse should correspond with the accents of the music, and that the inflexions of the reciting voice should be reproduced in the rise and fall of the music.

A common fault with beginners is the placing of unimportant words, such as " to " and " of ", on the accented beats of the music, with results such as the following :—

EXAMPLE 226

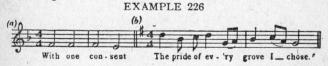

With one con-sent   The pride of ev-'ry grove I— chose.

If we scan

" Nearer, my God, to Thee, Nearer to Thee,"
it becomes clear that the metre of the poem almost
exactly corresponds to the accents of the hymn tune to
which it is set. Except in hymn tunes and Strophic
Songs,[1] however, the musical accents seldom coincide
with the actual metre of the words. The reason is best
explained by means of another example :—

" How sleep the brave, who sink to rest

By all their country's wishes blest ! "[2]

These lines, if set to music exactly as they are
scanned, might be treated thus :—

EXAMPLE 227

Such a treatment is both monotonous and unnatural,
for no actor who is worth his salt would dream of reading
or reciting in such a sing-song manner. Instead of
stressing every accented syllable in the metre he would
pass lightly over certain syllables thus :—

How sleep the brave, who sink to rest

By all their country's wishes blest ! "[2]

These lines might be treated musically as follows :—

EXAMPLE 228

---

[1] For an explanation of the Strophic Song, *see* page 225.
[2] Most lyrics may be set in either duple or triple time. In
some cases, such as this example, one is better than the other ;
in others it is often difficult to choose between them.

In setting words to music, therefore, the principal accents (*i.e.* those occurring when the poem is well recited) should coincide with the strong accents of the music ; the weaker syllables may then be treated in any way which seems artistically desirable.

The next point to be considered is the musical reproduction of the natural inflexions of the speaking voice. Since the poet cannot indicate the rise and fall of the words, it is the responsibility of the composer to interpret this. It is a good plan to mark the inflexions before the setting is begun, using the signs < and > to mark the rise and fall of the voice. Here is an example :—

>   <

" The Nightingale has been away,

>   >

But Spring again invites her."

From the example which follows you will see that these inflexions are reproduced in the music.

EXAMPLE 229

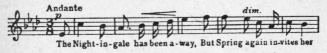

The Night-in-gale has been a-way, But Spring again in-vites her

It is scarcely necessary to say that the meaning of the words must be carefully considered. Such a setting as the following is ridiculous :—

EXAMPLE 230

Ris - ing   and fall - ing

Normally each syllable of a poem is set to a separate sound, short notes such as quavers and semiquavers being written with separate tails. Occasionally, however, two or more sounds are given to the same syllable, these notes being grouped together by a slur. An example of this occurs in the last bar of Example 228.

The Structure of Vocal Music

The form and style of vocal music is largely dependent on the words. The simplest form for a single voice is the **Strophic Song** in which each verse of a poem is set to the same melody. The majority of folk songs and national airs are strophic, as are many of the smaller songs of Schubert and Schumann, and numerous ballads. The Strophic Song is generally in simple Binary Form, often consisting of two eight-bar sentences. As in the hymn tune the musical accents usually coincide with the metre of the words. Since two or more verses are set to the same tune it is not always possible to avoid faulty accentuation. Sometimes, however, alterations, such as the allocation of two sounds to one syllable, must be made in the melody, to suit the changed accents of a particular verse.

In the example which follows the accentuation of the first verse is less satisfactory than that of the second.

EXAMPLE 231

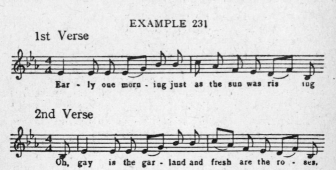

1st Verse

Ear - ly one morn - ing just as the sun was ris   ing

2nd Verse

Oh, gay   is the gar - land and fresh are the ro - ses.

Although the accompaniment to the Strophic Song sometimes remains the same throughout, it should generally be varied to suit the different character of each verse, and to avoid monotony.

Not all poems lend themselves to strophic treatment. The metre of one verse may differ from that of the other, or there may be a marked change of sentiment. When strophic treatment would be inappropriate, a poem is often set in simple or extended Ternary Form. Thus in a poem of three verses we often find that in the melody of the first and third verses is the same (with perhaps some variation in the accompaniment), but that the second verse is set to a new melody. The second melody is usually in some other key (which should be a related one), the third verse returning to the key of the Tonic. When the mood of the second verse is sadder or more reflective than that of the first, a change to the Relative Minor key is often effective.

In order to secure an effective finish to a song, a part of the last verse is sometimes repeated, thus :—

> " Yet this inconstancy is such
>   As thou, too, shalt adore ;
> I could not love thee, Dear, so much,
>   Loved I not Honour more.
> I could not love thee, Dear, so much,
>   Loved I not Honour more."

The sense of any such a repetition should always be complete. " Not Honour more, Not Honour more " is sheer nonsense. Another (and usually better) way of securing a good ending is by the augmentation of the final cadence (*see* Example 213, page 207).

Ballads of the more popular type sometimes consist of a verse and refrain (*i.e.* much the same form as the ordinary vocal fox-trot). The form is usually as follows :—

Introduction. 4 or 8 bars, often consisting of the last part of the refrain.

Verse. This often consists of three phrases, each 4 or 8 bars long. The first two phrases balance one another and make a complete sentence. The third forms a sort of Bridge Passage leading to the Refrain.

Refrain. 16 or 32 bars. Sometimes the end of the refrain is extended another 4 or 8 bars by a repetition of the final cadence.

If there are two verses followed by two refrains they may either be written out in full, or the sign D$ (from the sign) may be placed at the end of the first refrain, and $ at the beginning of the verse. The words of the second verse are then written underneath those of the first. If the refrain is to be repeated it must be provided with 1st and 2nd Time bars, the first leading back to the refrain, and the second providing a suitable ending to the song.

Piano Accompaniment

It is by no means easy to write a good piano accompaniment to a song. The accompaniment should suggest the character of the words in such a way that it does not distract the attention from the poem or the singer. A verse such as the following :—

" Piping down the valleys wild,
    Piping songs of pleasant glee,
On a cloud I saw a child,
    And he laughing said to me : "[1]

should be given a light, quick-moving accompaniment

---

[1] *Reeds of Innocence.* William Blake (1757-1827).

which reflects the carefree happiness of the child, and suggests, rather than imitates, the sound of the pipe. Light arpeggio or broken chord figures would clearly be more appropriate than sustained chords.

The quiet, contemplative mood of this verse:—

" And thou art dead, as young and fair
    As aught of mortal birth:
  And form so soft and charms so rare
    Too soon return'd to Earth ! "[1]

would best be reflected in an accompaniment of soft, slow-moving chords.

It is impossible to give examples of all the different styles of accompaniment. The beginner should study the songs of Schubert, whose accompaniments will repay the closest analysis.

In some songs the same style of accompaniment is maintained from beginning to end; in other, different verses are accompanied in different ways. It is important, however, that the style of accompaniment should be consistent; the following is simply ridiculous.

EXAMPLE 232

[1] *Elegy on Thyrza.* Lord Byron (1788-1824).

The melody of a song is often doubled in the accompaniment; this is especially common in ballads of a popular type. The doubling may be in the same octave as the voice, or in a higher or lower octave.

In studying methods of song accompaniment the following points should be borne in mind.

(1) A high voice is accompanied in the same way as a low voice. This means that although the pitch of a tenor is approximately an octave lower than that of a soprano, the difference need not be taken into account.

(2) The piano accompaniment should be complete in itself; that is to say, it should be satisfactory if the voice part is left out.

Introductions, Codas, and Interpolations

A song is generally preceded by a short Introduction for piano. This may consist simply of the accompaniment introduced a few bars ahead of the melody,[1] or of a phrase based either on some part of the melody or on a new idea. Occasionally some characteristic feature of the words is incorporated in the introductory bars of the music. The Introduction to Schubert's song *The Organ-Grinder*, for example, represents the drone bass and melody of the hurdy-gurdy, and that to his song *The Post*, the galloping of the postman's horses, and the sound of his horn.

Between the verses of a song there is usually an interpolated passage for piano, generally of from two to four bars in length; this is sometimes constructed from material used in the Introduction. There is often a similar break in the middle of the verse, but this should be very short, otherwise the continuity of the poem may be interrupted. Such a break is often valuable, firstly

[1] *See* Example 185, page 173.

to bring out more clearly the meaning of the words, and secondly to give the singer time to breathe.

In these lines, for instance,

" For what is left the poet here?
    For Greeks a blush—for Greece a tear."

the meaning would be made clearer if a slight break were made after the words " here " and " blush." In short, an interpolated passage should occur in the middle of a verse only when it is felt that a good actor would make a similar pause when reciting the poem.

A short Coda, often based on the last phrase of the melody, or on the Introduction, is usually added to a song to provide a satisfactory finish. During the Coda (or a part of it) a long note is sometimes sustained by the voice.

General Hints

The voice part of a solo song is generally written in the Treble Clef, whatever the voice for which it is intended. If sung by a soprano or contralto the notes will sound at their actual written pitch ; if sung by a tenor or bass they will sound an octave lower than written. In a hymn tune or a part-song, the soprano and contralto parts are written on the treble stave, and the tenor and bass parts on the bass stave ; the male voices then sound at their actual written pitch.

A song should be written as spontaneously as possible ; a melody which is constructed bar by bar is unlikely to flow easily and naturally. The two essentials of a successful song are a good melody and a good bass ; it is as well, therefore, to jot these down first of all, indicating the harmony by the symbols used in this book (I, V7c, and so on). Any polishing and trimming of the melody should take place before the accompaniment is added.

A song should be written for a particular voice, with the compass of that voice in mind. Songs are often transposed from the original key to suit other voices, but the effect is not the same.

Many songs have been written which are unvocal and, therefore, useless. The singer must make his own notes, and in doing so he has only his ear to guide him. The composer should therefore let his voice parts proceed smoothly, avoiding wide skips and awkward intervals. He must also remember that a consistently high or low tessitura imposes a strain on the voice which may cause bad tone and faulty intonation.

Exercises

The following poem may be set as a Strophic Song in $\frac{2}{4}$ time (*moderato*). A four-bar Introduction could also serve as an Interlude between the verses, and as a Coda. The accompaniment of at least two of the verses should be varied.

It was a Lover and his Lass

It was a lover and his lass,
 With a hey, and a ho, and a hey nonino,
That o'er the green corn-field did pass,
 In the spring time, the only pretty ring time,
When birds do sing, hey ding a ding, ding ;
· Sweet lovers love the spring.

Between the acres of the rye,
 With a hey, and a ho, and a hey nonino,
These pretty country folks would lie,
 In the spring time, the only pretty ring time,
When birds do sing, hey ding a ding, ding ;
Sweet lovers love the spring.

This carol they began that hour,
   With a hey, and a ho, and a hey nonino,
How that life was but a flower,
   In the spring time, the only pretty ring time,
When birds do sing, hey ding a ding, ding ;
Sweet lovers love the spring.

And therefore, take the present time,
   With a hey, and a ho, and a hey nonino,
For love is crowned with the prime,
   In the spring time, the only pretty ring time,
When birds do sing, hey ding a ding, ding ;
Sweet lovers love the spring.

                   William Shakespeare.

CHAPTER XXV

KEY, CHARACTER, AND EXPRESSION

The Choice of a Key

In choosing a suitable key for a particular composition, three factors must be taken into account.

(1) *The compass of the voice or instrument.* Vocal music must be written to suit some particular voice, or combination of voices, and the key chosen accordingly. It is usually best to begin by sketching out the cadence to the concluding words of the poem, as a striking close will often provide a clue to the most suitable key. In the key of C Major, for instance, the C's which lie within the normal range of the soprano voice are comparatively low and weak notes, and would only be suited to a quiet finish ; if a brilliant climax were desired the key of F or G Major should be chosen.

The compass of the piano is a wide one and need not be considered when choosing a key, but the small compass of some of the other instruments (*e.g.* Flute, Oboe, Clarinet) must be taken into account.

(2) *Standard of Difficulty.* The average performer of only moderate ability usually feels uncomfortable when playing or singing in a key with a signature of more than four sharps or flats. Ideally, sight-reading in all keys should be practised at an early stage ; as things are it is better to avoid the extreme keys unless the ability of the performer is known.

(3) *Key Colour.* Though it may be going too far to suggest that every major and minor key has a different mental effect, there can be no doubt that certain keys

are brighter than others. The choice of a key, therefore, must to some extent be conditioned by the sentiment of the music. Major keys are often chosen for expressing happiness and merriment, and minor keys for sadness and longing. Thus one would expect a *Valse Triste* or a *Funeral March* to be in a minor key rather than a major one. Though much lively music (*e.g.* many of the *Hungarian Dances* of Brahms) has been written in a minor key, it is generally pervaded by a sombre colouring.

Many writers have endeavoured to classify major and minor keys according to their different characteristics ; the results may be crystallized thus :—

Major Keys.

C	..	..	..	Bold, vigorous.
D flat	..	..	Sonorous, elegant.
D	..	..	..	Majestic, grand.
E flat	..	..	Dignified, soft.
E	..	..	..	Bright, powerful
F	..	..	..	Peaceful, contemplative.
F sharp	..	..	Brilliant, incisive.
G	..	..	..	Pastoral, gay.
A flat	..	..	Dreamy, gentle.
A	..	..	..	Confident, sunny.
B flat	..	..	Bright, graceful.
B	..	..	..	Energetic, bold.

Minor Keys.

C	..	..	..	Gloomy, sad.
C sharp	..	..	Tragic.
D	..	..	..	Solemn, subdued.
E flat	..	..	Very sombre.
E	..	..	..	Restless.

F ..	..	..	Gloomy, passionate.
F sharp	..	..	Mysterious, spectral.
G ..	..	..	Melancholy.
G sharp	..	..	Sorrowful, anxious.
A ..	..	..	Tender, noble.
B flat	..	..	Funereal.
B ..	..	..	Savage, ominous.

Although such a list can serve only as the roughest guide it may draw the attention of the beginner to the possibilities of key-colour. Many amateurs appear to have a predilection for a particular key or keys, from which they find difficulty in getting away. This practice, if persevered in, will lead to commonplace writing ; and the beginner should, therefore, train himself to vary the key according to the mood of the music.

Character and Emotion in Music

The principal object of the composer is to express his personal emotions, or those of others, or to attempt to interpret in sound real happenings or pictures that exist in the mind. The emotions or events which he endeavours to portray may broadly be classified under the following headings :—

    (a) Dance Music.
    (b) Fantasy.
    (c) Happiness (Friendship, Love, Triumph, etc.).
    (d) Humour.
    (e) Martial Music.
    (f) Religious Music.
    (g) Unemotional Descriptive Music (Pastoral, Storm, etc.).
    (h) Unhappiness (Despair, Gloom, Pain, etc.).

We shall now examine the means by which these subjects may be expressed in music, though it is clearly impossible to lay down any precise rules for their treatment.

FANTASY

The dancing of fairies, elves, and other sprites is usually depicted by a slender, rather artificial melody high up in the treble, with plenty of *staccato* notes. In piano music the hands are often placed rather far apart, though occasionally both hands play in the treble clef, producing a kind of " musical box " effect. Examples may be found in Tschaikowsky's *Dance of the Sugar-Plum Fairy* and *Reed-Pipe Dance* from the *Nutcracker* Suite, and Delibes's *Doll Dance* from the *Coppelia* Ballet.

HAPPINESS

Joy may be expressed by loud animated music with a melody which consists principally of arpeggio or broken chord figures, and simple harmonies; general merry-making and jollity demands bright music in $\frac{6}{8}$, $\frac{9}{8}$, or $\frac{12}{8}$ time. Examples may be found in Schumann's *The Merry Peasant*, and in such melodies as *Sir Roger de Coverley* and *Girls and Boys come out to play*. Love is portrayed by a flowing melody often moving principally by step, with occasional leaps of fairly large intervals.

EXAMPLE 233

Love Song at Sunset.   KING PALMER

(*Down a Country Lane*)

See also Liszt's *Liebestraum No. 3*, and Chopin's *Nocturne in E flat*.

HUMOUR

It is not easy to give a recipe for humour in music. One method is the introduction of some unusual interval in the melody, such as the drop of a major ninth (representing the braying of an ass) in the example which follows.

EXAMPLE 234

Overture (*A Midsummer Night's Dream*).   MENDELSSOHN

MARTIAL MUSIC

As marches are treated of in another chapter it is only necessary to add that the introduction of a bugle call or trumpet-like tune in a melody invariably produces a martial effect. Long accented notes with short unaccented ones following, in moderate $\frac{3}{4}$ or $\frac{4}{4}$ time, give an impression of stateliness and majesty.

RELIGIOUS MUSIC

It goes without saying that sacred music should be inspired by deep sincerity; nevertheless *Andante Religióso*, or some similar term, is often applied to music whose chief characteristic is a mawkish sentimentality. Good religious music tends towards simplicity and dignity; the beginner should study the sacred works of good modern composers.

UNEMOTIONAL DESCRIPTIVE MUSIC

There are so many different kinds of descriptive music that it is impossible to give any general characteristics.

Pastoral music is often written in moderate ⁶⁄₈ time, with a graceful melody and some form of Pedal Bass (*see* Example 199, page 191).

Music intended to depict a storm or a fire demands a quick-moving melody (usually in semiquavers), or some

EXAMPLE 235

Fire (*The Carnival of the Elements*).   HOWARD CARR
By permission of W. Paxton & Co., Ltd.

form of *tremolo* effect.   The music must continue without pause, the pitch rising or falling, and the music becoming louder or softer, as the storm (or fire) increases or decreases in fury.   Such music is usually written in a minor key.   The introduction of syncopation often adds to the effect.

UNHAPPINESS

Music expressing grief, gloom, anguish, or despair, is usually written in a minor key.   Perhaps the most characteristic feature of sad music is the frequent use of accented passing notes or suspensions—these dissonances (especially if they fall a minor second) are invariably pathetic in a minor key.

The poignancy of grief is greatly increased if the rhythm is restless and agitated, rather than smooth and tranquil.

EXAMPLE 236

Eine Trane (A Tear).   M. MOUSSORGSKY

Expression and Phrasing

If a composer wishes his music to be heard as he intends it to sound, he must be careful to put down, on paper, all the necessary marks of phrasing and expression, and indications of the pace and manner of performance.

The term indicating the pace or *tempo* at which the music is to be performed is placed over the first bar ; it may either stand alone, or it may be followed by a term describing the manner of performance. Thus *Moderato* means " at a moderate pace," and *Moderato e con energia* " at a moderate pace and with energy." Italian terms are generally used, as they are universally understood by musicians. A list of these terms may be found in any musical dictionary.

Phrasing is indicated by signs which show whether certain notes are to be played smoothly as a group, or detached from one another. The usual phrasing marks are as follows :—

(1) The *legato* mark (or slur). In piano music a curved line placed over or under two or more notes of different pitch indicates that they are to be played as smoothly as possible.

In string music a slur indicates that all the notes affected by it are to be played in the same movement of the bow.

It is not usual to insert *legato* marks in vocal music, but the slur is sometimes used when two or more notes are to be sung to one syllable.

(2) The *staccato* marks. A dot (*staccato*) placed over or under a note means that it is to be detached or separated from the next note. A note so marked is shortened by about half its length—thus a crotchet is made about as short as a quaver.

A note marked with a dash (*staccatissimo*) is made still shorter, being shortened by about three-quarters of its length.

When a slur is used in conjunction with dots (*mezzo-staccato*) the notes so marked are shortened by about a quarter of their length.

In studying the phrasing of piano music the following hints will be found useful.

(*a*) Sequences, and similar melodic and rhythmic patterns, should be phrased alike.

(*b*) A strong accent should usually be grouped with the weak accent which precedes it.

(*c*) A large leap often denotes the beginning of a fresh group of notes.

(*d*) A repeated note, or an abrupt change of tone-colour (*e.g.* from full to thin harmony) often begins a new group of notes.

Though no attempt need be made to indicate all the slight stresses and nuances which would be observed in the artistic performance of a work—this would defeat its own object as the notation would be hopelessly overladen—all major variations of speed, accent, and force should be accurately shown. In this the composer must be guided largely by his own instinct, though certain general principles may help him.

A *crescendo* (<), or an *accelerando* (a hastening of the *tempo*), implies increased excitement or intensification of effort ; a *diminuendo* (>), or a *rallentando* (a slackening of the *tempo*), the reverse. A *rallentando* when combined with a *crescendo* is commonly used when the music rises to a climax, and a *diminuendo* when the climatic point has been passed.

A note or chord requiring special emphasis (*sforzando*) can be marked with the sign > or *sf*. When a sudden drop in the quantity of tone is required, *fp* (*forte-piano*) may be used. Long high notes which form a climax may be prolonged by means of a pause (⌒), but as the pause interrupts the flow of the music it should be used only with some definite purpose in mind.

CHAPTER XXVI

FORMS IN MUSICAL COMPOSITION

Musical compositions may conveniently be divided into three general classes or styles:

(1) **VOCAL.** This class includes such compositions as the Ballad, Chant, Hymn, and Song.

(2) **INSTRUMENTAL.** This class includes short pieces such as the Barcarolle, Impromptu, Intermezzo, and March.

(3) **DANCE.** This class includes dances such as the Fox-trot, Gavotte, Mazurka, and Waltz.

The forms described in this chapter are limited to those which lie within the scope of this book. The larger forms—Opera, Cantata, Symphony, Concerto, for example—are not therefore included. Some aspects of certain compositions (e.g. Chant, Hymn, March, and Waltz) have already been discussed in other chapters. It is only possible to indicate the framework of the various forms; the details must be filled in by reference to actual musical examples.

Throughout this chapter the letters A, B, C, and D are used to represent the different periods for which a composition is made up.

Air (French), *Ayre* (English). In the late sixteenth and early seventeenth centuries, this was a general term applied to a song. During the eighteenth century the name was often given to a melodious movement of a suite (e.g. Bach's *Partitas* Nos. 4 and 6, and his *French Suite* No. 4, contain Airs).

Album Leaf. From the German *Albumblätt*. A title sometimes given to a short instrumental piece, in any form, such as might be written in an autograph album. Schumann's *Albumblätter*, Op. 124, is a collection of twenty short pieces.

Anthem. A vocal composition, usually with organ accompaniment. The words are generally taken from the Psalms, or from some other portion of the Scriptures or Liturgy. The form varies according to the requirements of the text. The anthem, which was created by the Anglican Church, is the one part of the service which is reserved for the choir, the congregation taking no part.

Arabesque (French). A title used by Schumann, Debussy and others for fanciful, characteristic pieces in which there is much ornamentation of the melody.

Aria (Italian). From the eighteenth century onwards this had come to mean a well-developed vocal solo, with instrumental accompaniment, consisting of three sections, the third section being identical with the first. The name has also been given to an instrumental movement with a well-defined " air ".

Aubade (French). Morning music, in distinction to the *Serenade*, which is evening music. The title is applied to a short vocal or instrumental piece of a melodious, and usually sentimental, character.

Badinage (French). An instrumental piece of a light and playful character.

Bagatelle (French). Literally, " a trifle ". A short piece, usually for the piano, which is written in a simple, light style.

Ballad. Originally a song used as an accompaniment to a dance, the word Ballad has been used in nearly all ages in a loose and vague sense. The true ballad is of an epic character—a song that tells a story. It consists of a series of four-line verses, of which the second and fourth lines usually finish with a silent beat.

> " In Scarlet town, where I was born,
>   There was a fair maid dwellin',
> Made every youth cry *Well-a-way!*
>   Her name was Barbara Allen. "

The modern ballad is more often derived from the so-called " drawing-room " ballad of Victorian times, and is simply a light or sentimental song, almost invariably consisting of three verses. (For the form of this kind of ballad see Chapter XXIV.) The term is also applied to the more melodious type of vocal dance tune; e.g. Ballad Fox-trot.

Ballade. A name given to an instrumental piece which is supposed to be based on a narrative. The music, which may be written in any form, should possess the heroic spirit of the true ballad. The finest examples are Chopin's *Ballades* for piano, Op. 23, 38, 47, 52. Brahms, Liszt, Grieg, and others have also left specimens.

Barcarolle (French). A vocal or instrumental piece in imitation of the songs composed by the Venetian gondoliers. The music is nearly always in $\frac{6}{8}$ time (moderate pace), with a simple and tranquil melody, and the regular alternation of heavy and light beats, suggestive of the motion of oars. There is no set form. Well-known examples are Chopin's *Barcarolle*, Op. 60 (probably the only specimen in $\frac{12}{8}$ time), Offenbach's *Barcarolle* from *The Tales of Hoffman*, and Mendelssohn's

Venetianisches Gondellied, Op. 19, No. 6, and Op. 62, No. 29.

Berceuse (French).   A lullaby or cradle song.   The title is generally applied to a quiet instrumental piece in $\frac{6}{8}$ time, with a simple melody and a lulling, rocking accompaniment.   The entire piece is often based on the Tonic Pedal; Chopin's *Berceuse*, Op. 57, for piano, is a remarkable example.   The accompaniment to Brahms's exquisite little song *Wiegenlied* (German for " cradle song ") is also based on the Tonic Pedal throughout.

Bolero (Spanish).   A lively Spanish dance performed at a moderate speed in $\frac{3}{4}$ or $\frac{3}{8}$ time.   The melody is usually sung by the dancers and accompanied by castanets in the following characteristic rhythm, which frequently begins a bar or more before the melody:

The form usually consists of two regular periods (of eight or sixteen bars) and a Trio.   The dance is intended to represent a love-story, starting with coyness and diffidence, and gradually working up to passionate ecstasy; the music should therefore increase in intensity as the dance proceeds.

The form of the instrumental bolero not intended for dancing is less regular; Chopin's *Bolero in A Minor*, for instance, begins with two five-bar phrases.   The most popular bolero of recent times is that by Ravel, which consists of what is virtually a single *crescendo* for orchestra, lasting about seventeen minutes.

Cachucha (Spanish).   A Spanish dance in $\frac{3}{4}$ or $\frac{3}{8}$ time which closely resembles the *Bolero* (q.v.), except that it is danced by a single performer instead of by couples. Perhaps the most familiar example is Gilbert and Sullivan's *Dance a Cachucha* from *The Gondoliers*.

Canzona or *Canzone* (Italian). Originally a form of song-poem sung by the Troubadors and Minstrels. In modern use the name is sometimes given to an instrumental piece with a song-like melody. There is no set form.

Carol. The word Carol, which possibly has its origin in the mediaeval " carole ", a round dance with vocal accompaniment, has come to mean a song of joy, exultation, and devotion to be sung at Christmas.

Cavatina (Italian). (1) A short simple song of one movement only. (2) A short instrumental piece with a slowish, graceful melody; Raff's *Cavatina* for violin and piano is a popular example.

Chant. The short simple melodies to which the psalms are set. A single Anglican chant consists of a single sentence made up of a three-bar and a four-bar phrase, the two phrases overlapping. A double chant contains two sentences built on the same plan. The first note of each phrase is called the *reciting note*, and is continued *ad libitum* while the words are recited; the cadence which follows is sung in strict time.

Characteristic Piece. A name sometimes applied to a light instrumental composition of no set form, and usually of a descriptive character.

Cortège (French). Literally " procession ". An instrumental piece with a solemn or triumphal march-like character.

Czardas or *Csárdás*. An Hungarian national dance

in two parts—a *Lassú*, a slow and sad movement (*andante*) in $\frac{2}{4}$ or $\frac{3}{4}$ time, and a *Friss*, a lively and fiery movement (*allegro vivace* or *presto*) in $\frac{2}{4}$ time. The first part is usually in a minor key, and the second in the key of the Tonic Major. Liszt wrote *Czardas Obstiné* and *Czardas Macabre* for piano.

Duet. Any composition for two voices or instruments; also a composition for two performers, either at the same piano or at two instruments.

Elegy. An instrumental or vocal composition of a plaintive, mournful character.

Entr'acte (French). Literally " between the acts ". A piece of music performed between the acts of a play or opera.

Étude (French). A study; any composition intended to give practice in some special difficulty. In the hands of Chopin, Debussy, and others this executive purpose was combined with music of great beauty.

Fox-trot. This American ballroom dance (dating from about 1915), is written in ₵ time, and is played at a slow or moderate speed. It usually consists of one or more verses and a chorus. The form of the average song copy (i.e. a copy showing the voice line, words, accompaniment, guitar symbols, and formerly notation for ukulele and tonic sol-fa) is as follows:—

Introduction: 4 bars (often the last four bars of the chorus).
Verse: 8, 12, or 16 bars.
Chorus: 32 bars (with 1st and 2nd time endings).

The form of the chorus is usually A (8 bars), A (8

bars), B (8 bars), A (8 bars). Sometimes the last sentence is extended for a further four bars by delaying the final cadence.

A form similar to the above has been used for many different varieties of modern popular songs and dances.

Galop or *Galopade* (French). A very lively dance in $\frac{2}{4}$ time consisting of quick, springing movements. It originated in Germany, and became fashionable in England and France during the early nineteenth century. After a time it was introduced in the *Quadrille* (q.v.), and ceased to be an independent dance. There is often an Introduction and a Coda, and one or two Trios.

Gavotte (French). A French dance of a lively but dignified character which became very popular at the Court of Louis XIV, its Paris vogue lasting until the French Revolution. The dance is performed at a moderate pace, and is written in ¢ time. It consists of two periods (i.e. simple Binary Form), each beginning at the half-bar with two crotchets, and ending at the half-bar with a minim. Often each section is repeated. Sullivan introduced a vocal gavotte into *The Gondoliers*.

Hornpipe. Originally the name of a musical instrument which was presumably fashioned from the horn of some animal, the name Hornpipe is now given to a rollicking sailors' step dance in $\frac{4}{4}$ time. The form is simple Binary; two periods, each of which is repeated.

Hymn. A song of praise or adoration to the deity, divided into verses, and used in the religious services of almost every cult. Although hymn tunes are generally written in four-part harmony, the melody is normally sung in unison by the congregation. It follows, therefore, that the melody should possess individuality and attractiveness when sung in unison without any accompaniment; it should also lie well within the compass of the average voice (i.e. approximately from middle C to E in the highest space of the treble stave—male voices sounding an octave lower). This does not, of course, mean that the harmony is unimportant. There must be good workmanship throughout; a strong bass, and inner parts which, as far as possible, have some melodic interest of their own.

Verses for hymn tunes are written in varied metres. In many hymn books the number of syllables in the lines is shown by means of figures, thus facilitating the fitting of the tunes to the words. Thus 86.86, known as Common Metre (C.M.), has a long note at the end of the second and fourth lines. The verse which follows is written in this metre.

" O God, our help in ages past,	8
Our hope for years to come,	6
Our shelter from the stormy blast,	8
And our eternal home."	6

66.86, known as Short Metre (S.M.), has a long note at the end of the first, second, and fourth lines, the third line continuing without a break. Long Metre (L.M.), 88.88, is entirely without breaks. There are also other less common metres. The composer who wishes to go further into the matter should study *Songs of Praise Discussed* compiled by Percy Dearmer (Oxford University Press) which contains much useful information relating to hymn prosody.

Idyll. A short instrumental composition in a pastoral style.

Impromptu (French). Literally a piece composed

without previous consideration or planning. The term is used for piano compositions which are written in a free style and in a form which varies according to the whim of the composer. The finest examples are the *Impromptus* of Chopin, especially that in F Sharp Major, Op. 36. Schubert composed two sets of *Impromptus*, Op. 90 and 142.

Intermezzo (Italian). Originally a dramatic or musical interlude introduced between the acts of an opera or play. Nowadays the term is often applied to short independent compositions (e.g. Schumann's *Six Intermezzi*, Op. 4, and Brahm's *Three Intermezzi*, Op. 117).

The name Intermezzo is frequently given to light piano pieces of a graceful and melodious character. These are usually written in $\frac{4}{4}$ time, and the form is often as follows:—

Introduction, A, B, A, C, A, B, A, Coda.

Each period is generally 16 bars long, and the Introduction and Coda from 2 to 8 bars long.

Jig (English), *Gigue* (French), *Giga* (Italian). The English Jig, a popular dance of the sixteenth century, is thought to have been the forerunner of the French Gigue and the Italian Giga. The French type is a lively dance, usually with a $\frac{6}{8}$ or $\frac{6}{4}$ time signature and a dotted rhythm, while the Italian type is quicker, and has fast running passages built on a simple harmonic foundation.

Lancers. A set of Quadrilles (q.v.).

Ländler (German). A species of slow, rustic waltz, in $\frac{3}{8}$ or $\frac{3}{4}$ time, peculiar to certain parts of Austria and the Tyrol. The melody is written in a simple style, quaver movement predominating.   Ländler have been written by Mozart, Beethoven, Schubert, and other German composers.

March.   A form of composition originally associated with military movements, but now more often written for the stage or concert hall.   The characteristic quality of all marches is a well-marked rhythm, and they are therefore very much akin to the so-called Dance Forms (Minuet and Trio, Mazurka, etc.). Marches may be divided into three main classes: the *Quick* March, the *Grand* March, and the *Funeral* March.

(1) *The Quick March*, or *Quickstep*.   This kind of march, which may be written in $\frac{2}{4}$, ₵, or $\frac{6}{8}$ time, is well exemplified in Sousa's *Washington Post*, Alford's *Colonel Bogey*, and Eric Coates's *Knightsbridge*.   The form is usually Ternary, but differs in dimensions.   At its simplest the modern Quick March consists of two periods followed by a Trio.   The following is a typical construction:—

Introduction (4 bars) ‖: A (16 bars) :‖: B (16 bars) :‖ ‖: Trio C (16 bars) :‖: D (16 bars) :‖

The Trio ends with a *Da Capo*, the Introduction, A, and B being played again.   It is customary to omit the repeats when returning to the first two periods after the *Da Capo*.

The first part of the march should be of a vigorous and strongly rhythmic character; the Trio smoother and more gently flowing.   Sometimes the Trio is preceded by a short Introduction (usually two bars of accompaniment).   Occasionally there is a short Coda.

The form of Sousa's *Washington Post* march is as follows:—

Introduction (8 bars) ‖: A (16 bars) :‖: B (16 bars) :‖
‖: C (16 bars) :‖: Bridge Passage (8 bars); C (16 bars) :‖.

Many of Sousa's other marches follow the construction first mentioned, except that there is no *Da Capo*.

(2) *The Grand March*. This kind of march also goes under the name of *Slow* or *Festival March*. Marches of this class include Mendelssohn's *Wedding March*, German's *Coronation March* from *Henry VIII*, and Elgar's *Pomp and Circumstance Marches*. They are generally written in $\frac{4}{4}$ time (occasionally in $\frac{2}{4}$), and are played at a slower tempo than the Quick March. For marching purposes the speed of the two kinds of marches is defined as: Slow March about 75 steps to the minute; Quick March about 120 steps to the minute.

(3) *The Funeral March*, or *Dead March*. This is slow and solemn in character. The first part is generally in the minor key, and the Trio in the major. Well-known examples are the Funeral Marches of Beethoven (Op. 26), Schubert (Op. 40), and Chopin.

Mazurka (German). A Polish national dance in $\frac{3}{4}$ or $\frac{3}{8}$ time, and considerably slower than the Waltz. Characteristic features are an emphasis on the second beat of the bar, the end of the phrases on that beat (i.e. feminine endings), and the division of the first beat into two melody notes, the first of which is usually dotted. The following are typical rhythms:—

The usual form is a first part of 8 or 16 bars, followed by a Trio of the same length, each part being repeated, but the larger mazurkas are in simple Ternary Form. The earliest mazurkas were frequently constructed on a Pedal Bass, generally the Tonic. The 52 *Mazurkas* of Chopin provide the finest examples.

Minuet. An old French dance in $\frac{3}{4}$ time; originally slow and stately, it later quickened in pace and altered in character. The usual form is simple Ternary—the first part, the Trio, and the first part repeated.

Mode. The only meaning of this word which need be considered here is that which is applied to the eight different kinds of scale which were devised during the fourth and sixth centuries by Ambrose, Bishop of Milan, and Pope Gregory. The eight modes made be heard by playing eight consecutive white keys on the piano, starting first on C, and then on D, E, F, G, A, and B. Although the only mode that we recognise today is that starting on C, some of the other modes have been used by modern composers, notably Vaughan Williams.

Morceau (French). A title sometimes given to a short, unpretentious piece. There is no set form.

Moto Perpetuo (Italian). A piece which proceeds throughout in quick notes.

Nocturne (French). A composition (usually instrumental) suggestive of the night; a serenade. There is no set form, but the tempo is usually slow, and the melody light and graceful. There is often some form of broken chord or arpeggio accompaniment. The nocturne was originated by the Irish composer, John Field, and perfected by Chopin, who left 19 *Nocturnes*.

Novelette. An instrumental movement of a romantic character.

Ostinato (Italian). A phrase which is repeated persistently throughout a composition, or a section of one. The Basso Ostinato, or Ground Bass, is usually a four-bar or eight-bar phrase, which is constantly repeated as a bass line, while the upper parts are varied.

Paso Doble (Spanish). Literally " double step." A lively dance in $\frac{6}{8}$ or $\frac{3}{4}$ time which became popular during the first quarter of the present century. A Paso Doble in $\frac{2}{4}$ or $\frac{6}{8}$ time is sometimes called a *Spanish March*.

Pastorale (French) or *Pastoral* (English). An instrumental composition, usually in $\frac{6}{8}$ or $\frac{12}{8}$ time, in a pastoral or rural style.

Polka. A lively Bohemian dance in $\frac{2}{4}$ time, which originated in the first half of the nineteenth century. It is written in regular four-bar phrases with the characteristic rhythm:—

Polacca (see *Polonaise*).

Polonaise (French), or *Polacca* (Italian). A Polish national dance in $\frac{3}{4}$ time which is performed at a moderate tempo (*Allegro moderato* or *Allegro maestoso*). Characteristic features are a strong emphasis on the second beat of the bar, the ending of the phrases on the third beat (i.e. feminine ending), and the accompanying

rhythm

The original form was simple Binary, but Chopin, whose *Polonaises* were a vital expression of his own national feeling, adopted Ternary Form (often considerably extended).

Pot-pourri (French).   A selection or medley of various tunes; thus a pot-pourri on melodies from *Rigoletto*, and so on.

Prelude.   Originally a piece of music to be played as an introduction.   From the nineteenth century, however, the term was used by Chopin, Debussy, and others as a title for a short instrumental piece, usually for piano.

Quadrille (French).   A dance which became very popular in France during the early part of the eighteenth century and was brought to England in 1816 by Lady Jersey.   It takes its name from the squares formed by the dancers who face each other in couples.   The quadrille consists of five consecutive movements.

1. *Le Pantalon* ($\frac{6}{8}$ time).
2. *L'Été* ($\frac{2}{4}$ time).
3. *La Poule* ($\frac{6}{8}$ time).
4. *La Trenise* and *La Pastourelle* ($\frac{2}{4}$ time).
5. *La Finale* consisting of three parts repeated four times.

Each of the first four parts consists of 32 bars, the dance beginning at the ninth bar.   The *Lancers*, danced by eight or sixteen couples, is a variant of the quadrille.

Reel.   A dance in quick $\frac{4}{4}$ time, usually consisting of four- or eight-bar phrases which are repeated several times.

Rhapsody.   A composition of no regular form, and generally of a brilliant, showy nature.   It often consists of a string of popular melodies, folk tunes, or national songs, loosely connected together. Examples are the *Hungarian Rhapsodies* of Liszt, and the *Rhapsody in Blue* of George Gershwin.

Romance (French), *Romanza* (Italian). (1) A short instrumental piece of a lyrical character. (2) A French love song.

Rumba (Spanish). A Cuban dance in ₵ time, played at a moderate speed. It is usually accompanied by maracas (hollow shells filled with seeds), claves (round sticks of hard wood which are struck together), bongoes (small Cuban drums), and a gourd (which emits a peculiar rubbing sound), all playing in different rhythms. The characteristic bass rhythm is

Saltarello (Italian). A lively Italian dance, usually in $\frac{6}{8}$ or $\frac{12}{8}$ time.

Samba (Portuguese). A lively Brazilian dance in $\frac{2}{4}$ time, with syncopated rhythms.

Sarabande (French). A stately dance (seventeenth and eighteenth centuries) in slow triple time.

Scherzo (Italian). Originally used to replace the third movement (minuet) in classical symphonies and chamber music. The scherzo, like the minuet, was followed by a contrasted section (trio), after which the scherzo was repeated. Later, the term was often applied to a quick movement in $\frac{3}{4}$ time (e.g. Scherzo from *A Midsummer Night's Dream* by Mendelssohn).

Schottische. A Scottish round dance in $\frac{2}{4}$ time. The music is similar to that of the *Polka* (q.v.), but is played rather slower.

Seguidilla (Spanish).   A lively dance of southern Spain in moderately fast triple time.

Serenade (French). Evening music.   (1) A short vocal or instrumental piece of a light and sentimental character, such as might be sung or played by a lover beneath his lady's window.   (2) A light, pleasing instrumental composition consisting of several movements.

Siciliano (Italian).   A pastoral dance in $\frac{6}{8}$ or $\frac{12}{8}$ time, originating in Sicily; a lyrical melody is usually accompanied by a swaying rhythm.

Sketch.   This title is sometimes applied to a short piece, usually for piano, of slight construction and no set form.

Song.   Strictly speaking, the name Song embraces every kind of vocal composition in which music is set to words.   In practice, its application is generally limited to a short composition for one or more voices, with or without accompaniment.   Songs may be classified under a large number of different headings (e.g. Love, Humorous, Sacred, Patriotic, Drinking, and Hunting songs).   The characteristics of each may be studied in the songs of Schubert, Schumann, Wolf, Grieg, Quilter, Coates, and others.   Song form is considered in Chapter XXIV.

Spanish March.   See *Paso Doble*.

Strathspey.   A slow Scottish dance in $\frac{4}{4}$ time, a characteristic feature of which is the " Scotch Snap " (a dotted note preceded by a shorter note).

Study.   See *Étude*.

Suite.   A series of separate movements or pieces. At the time of Bach and Handel the suite consisted of four dance movements—Allemande, Courante, Sarabande, and Gigue—to which other movements (e.g. Prelude, Bourrée, and Gavotte) were frequently added. The modern Suite consists of several short contrasted movements, not necessarily in dance form, in varied keys. Some suites are associated with a definite " programme ", and descriptive titles are given to each movement (e.g. *Summer Days* Suite by Eric Coates); others are made up of movements selected from ballets or from incidental music to plays.

Tango.   A modern dance of Spanish-American origin in $\frac{2}{4}$ time, which is danced at a slow walking pace. Characteristics are a slow, nostalgic melody, often in a minor key, accompanied by a rhythm such as $\frac{2}{4}$ ♪♪♪ ♪♪ or ♪♪♪ ♪♪ , and a feminine final cadence thus, ♪♪ ♪ , In addition to the genuine tango, there are pseudo varieties such as the Tango-Foxtrot, a cross between the two dances, which is usually written in ₵ time.

Tarantella (Italian).   A Neapolitan dance of very quick tempo (*presto*) in $\frac{6}{8}$ time.   It may have received its name from the tarantula, a large spider whose bite was said to be curable only by dancing until overcome by fatigue.   The melody of the tarantella generally moves continuously in quavers; the form is usually Ternary.

Waltz.   A popular dance in $\frac{3}{4}$ time, almost certainly of German origin.   The tempo of the waltz may be either quick, moderate or slow; the melody is generally smooth and flowing, and may be in either a major or a minor key. A characteristic feature is that there is usually only one harmony in a bar, the bass of the chord being sounded on the first beat, and the rest of the chord on the second and third beats (see Example 38, Chapter III).

The Waltz may or may not be designed for dancing, and the form varies accordingly. At its simplest, it is written in simple Binary Form. Thus Brahms's *Waltz in G Major*, Op. 39, No. 10, consists of two periods of 8 bars, each repeated. More elaborate waltzes are generally written in Ternary Form and include a Trio (usually in the key of the subdominant). Chopin's *Waltz in D Flat Major*, Op. 70, No. 3, is constructed on the following plan:—

||: A (8 bars) :||: B (8 bars) :||: TRIO C (8 bars) :||
FINE
||: D (8 bars) :||: C (8 bars) :||:
D.C.

Quick waltzes intended for dancing are often written in sets of four or five short waltzes, usually consisting of either two or three sixteen-bar sentences. These waltzes are preceded by an Introduction, which need not be in $\frac{3}{4}$ time, and followed by a Coda in which the principal melodies are repeated. In this Coda it is not unusual to find the cadences of the various melodies overlapping, so as to avoid any pause in the music.

CHAPTER XXVII

THE BUSINESS SIDE OF MUSICAL COMPOSITION

Originality and Plagiarism

Mr. Percy Scholes, in his *Oxford Companion to Music*, suggests that there are two distinct qualities passing under the title of originality. The first he calls " actual novelty in melody, harmony, form, etc.", and the second " a strong expression of personality allied to a high degree of craftsmanship ". Originality of the first kind is found only in those who have discovered some new form or style of music, and to these men every composer who possesses the second kind of originality is indebted. Thus Field's claim to originality rests on his creation of a new musical form which he called *Nocturne*, and though Field's music is now neglected, Chopin undoubtedly owed him a considerable debt when he composed music in a similar style.

Many of the great composers have borrowed ideas from the works of other composers, or from folk tunes and other national music. Handel, in particular, has been criticized for his frequent borrowings. The composer who borrows from folk music[1] deserves reproach as little as the author who borrows from traditional legends and fairy tales, for these belong to the world and anyone is free to make what use of them he will. But to borrow from another composer's works is a very different thing. The late Mr. Carl Engel once said that " it would be unreasonable to regard such a plagiarism

---

[1] Some folk music may be copyright (e.g. if it has been arranged by a composer whose works are still in copyright).

as a theft unless the plagiarist conceals the liberty he is taking by disguising the appropriation so as to make it appear a creation of his own ", adding, " some inferior musicians display much talent in this procedure ". There are, of course, legitimate purposes for which borrowed themes may be used—Brahms, for instance, wrote variations on themes taken from Haydn, Schumann, and others.   Composers have also made transcriptions or arrangements of the works of other composers—thus a song may be adapted as a piano piece, orchestral music arranged for the organ, and so on. Although modern opinion tends to condemn arrangements, it ought surely to be allowed that an arrangement which preserves the spirit of the original composition must be of some artistic value.   Much more deserving of condemnation is the borrowing of melodies from the great masters by composers of dance music.   Themes from the works of Mozart, Schubert, Schumann, Chopin, Liszt, and Tchaikovsky have all been maltreated in this way.

No composer has ever gained much by deliberately imitating someone else's ideas.   " The misfortune of the imitator ", says Schumann, " is that he can only appropriate the salient points of his original; an involuntary awe disables him from copying its peculiar beauties."   In borrowing and adapting from the works of others, the composer must be guided not only by his artistic conscience, but also by the law of copyright. The provisions of this law are explained in another section of this chapter, and it is only necessary to add that any unauthorized use of a copyright work constitutes an infringement.   Copyright is infringed only if a *substantial part* of the work is copied, but this must be taken to mean a vital part, not necessarily a large part.

The copying of only a few bars might be deemed an infringement if it could be proved that they were an original and vital part of the work. This is a point of some importance, as many people have the mistaken idea that so many consecutive bars of music (usually four) may be copied without infringement of copyright.

Copyright may sometimes be innocently infringed by a composer who is quite unconscious of any plagiarism. When listening to the music of some other composer the ear may be attracted towards some particular phrase or progression; this is stored in the memory and later reproduced under the impression that it has been freshly created. In the early stages you will probably commit a good deal of unconscious plagiarism, but as this music is unlikely to be published or performed in public, little harm will be done. As I have said, originality will only come with experience. Plagiarism is especially likely to occur in melodies of the " ear-tickling " variety (e.g. dance tunes and musical comedy numbers); but many of the phrases which make up this kind of music are so hackneyed that they almost amount to clichés, and it is doubtful whether copyright could be claimed for them.

You must take every effort to avoid plagiarism, but having done so you need not worry unduly over the possibility of committing some accidental breach of copyright which may involve you in a legal action. If your music is published, then the publisher, in his own interest, will take steps to prevent any possible infringement of copyright; if your music is unpublished and you wish to assure yourself of its originality, ask your musical friends, especially any who are themselves aspiring composers, to point out the " reminiscences ". This is a task they will undertake gladly, and perhaps not without some relish.[1]

Copyright

British copyright in a musical work subsists during the life of the composer and for a period of fifty years after his death.[2] Copyright in a work published posthumously subsists for a period of fifty years either from the date of publication or from the date of the first performance, whichever is the earlier. This period also applies in certain foreign countries; others, including the U.S.A., have different terms of copyright.[3] Let us see how this works out in practice. Sterndale Bennett died in 1875; all his compositions which were published during his lifetime are therefore non-copyright, and anyone is free to make whatever use of them he likes. Sir Edward Elgar died in 1934; the music published during his lifetime will therefore be copyright until 1984, and no one may make use of it before that date without the permission of the owner of the copyright.

The term copyright covers the rights of (1) publication, (2) public performance, (3) mechanical reproduction and broadcast transmission. Copyright may exist in the arrangement of a non-copyright work. Even the

---

[1] Some busy professional composers do arrange insurance cover against accidental infringement of copyright. Cases are rarely brought, as infringement of musical copyright is usually difficult to prove, and actions can be very costly. Alleged infringements, however, are often settled out of court, by arrangements between the composers and publishers concerned.

[2] This term of copyright also applies to literary works. Thus the words of a song remain copyright for fifty years after the author's death, irrespective of whether or not the copyright of the music has expired

[3] The original term of copyright in the U.S.A. is twenty-eight years; this may be renewed on expiration for a further period of the same length.

editing of non-copyright music (e.g. the fingering and phrasing of a piano piece) may be copyrighted as original work. In order to ascertain whether or not a published work is copyright, therefore, it is necessary to find out (a) the date of the composer's death, (b) the date of publication, and (c) whether the printed copy has been arranged or edited. In the latter case it is often possible to trace the original edition in the music library of the British Museum.

No special steps need be taken by the composer of an unpublished work; so long as he keeps the music unpublished the copyright remains his absolutely and for all time. In the event of a breach the owner may bring an action for damages, penalties, or an injunction, though such an action is seldom worth while as breach of copyright in a musical work is often difficult to prove. When a work is accepted for publication the composer, in consideration of certain agreed royalties and fees, assigns the copyright to the publishers, who then secure international copyright by filing the statutory number of copies at the British Museum Copyright Office and in the Library of Congress at Washington.

There is no exclusive copyright in a title, but to avoid confusion and possible ill-feeling it is naturally inadvisable to choose a title which has already been used by another composer.

Music Publishing

As to publishing music, let me start with a warning. From time to time mushroom publishing firms appear—and disappear with a substantial harvest gathered from composers who are eager to see their efforts in print. The method is a simple one. An advertisement—often under some high-sounding name

—is inserted (usually in the provincial press) inviting composers and lyric writers to submit compositions of all kinds with a view to publication. In answer to this advertisement an enthusiastic composer submits, let us say, a song, and is then informed that it has been carefully considered, and with some slight revision should achieve considerable success. The composer forwards the fee for the revision (perhaps £5), and in due course receives a revised copy of his composition together with an offer of publication. This suggests that the composer should pay a sum of £30 (or more) towards the cost of printing and "exploitation", in return for which he will receive a substantial royalty on copies sold (the publishers can afford to be generous since no copies will be sold) and a share of mechanical and broadcast fees. If he is foolish enough to send the money he receives, after a protracted correspondence, either a few copies of his song, badly printed on cheap paper (at a cost of £10 or less), or a returned postal packet marked "Gone away". In my early days I was myself bitten by one of these sharks, and ever since I have warned composers not to waste their money. But it is surprising how often the advice has gone unheeded.

If for any reason a composer wishes to have one of his compositions printed at his own expense, he should approach a reputable firm of music publishers who undertake such work; they will charge him a fair price, and will give him any editorial assistance he may require. The cost of engraving (or photographing, etc.) and printing should not be heavy, but unless the composer is able to sell a substantial number of copies to his friends and supporters, the transaction is not likely to show a profit.

With the advent of the modern "pop" song, the

success of which depends almost entirely on whether or not the publisher is able to obtain successful recordings, a new harvest is being gathered in by certain small firms who offer " to make a record of your song by a popular artist " for submission to publishers. If a composer is so convinced of the merit of his song that he is willing to pay for a recording on disc or tape, he should make his own arrangements with one of the many reputable companies which make private recordings; even though the chances of success in placing the song may be the same (nil), the cost will at least be far lighter. In this connection, if the composer has a tape-recorder and can produce a tolerable recording of his music, he may find that certain publishers are willing to listen to the tape. In the field of popular music this may be a considerable advantage, since the choice of music for publication is often made by people who cannot read music and, moreover, may wish to ask someone in a record company to hear the tape. On the other hand, more serious music is usually selected for publication only after the actual musical score has been considered by experienced musicians.

In the normal course of events, a publisher who likes a composition which has been submitted to him, and who has room for it in his catalogue, will offer either to buy it outright or to publish it on a royalty basis. A small composition, such as a hymn tune or an arrangement of a non-copyright work, is often bought for an outright payment of a few pounds. A song or piano piece is more often published on a royalty basis. The usual terms are a 10 per cent. royalty on sheet sales, and 50 per cent. of performing rights and mechanical fees. There may, or may not, be a small advance payment on account of royalties.

Publication on a royalty basis is the most equitable method, for, if the work is a success, both the composer and the publisher reap the benefit, but if the beginner is offered an outright payment he may do well to accept it, as once he has broken the ice he is more likely to secure better terms.

It might seem unnecessary to say that any composition which is submitted to a publisher should be legibly written on twelve-stave music paper, were it not that some amateur composers send in manuscripts scrawled in pencil, and either too small to be read or too large to be placed on the music desk. A stamped, addressed envelope should always be enclosed with the manuscript, and a rough copy kept in case of loss.

If several copies of a composition are needed, it may be worth while to have these photo-copied. This is cheaper and quicker than professional hand-copying, and if a clear and correct original is provided (preferably written in black ink), the composer can be assured that no new errors have found their way into the copies.

A composition may be rejected for two reasons other than lack of merit: (1) the publisher may be overstocked with that kind of music, or (2) the manuscript may have been sent to the wrong publisher. A composition which has been refused can always be submitted elsewhere, but it is essential to study the catalogues of the various publishers so as to discover the most suitable markets.

The Performing Right Society

The Performing Right Society Ltd. (29/33, Berners Street, London W.1) is an association of composers, lyric authors, and music publishers, established to collect fees for the public performance of copyright

musical works, and to restrain the unauthorized performance of such works, both in this country and
abroad. The Society controls all kinds of vocal and
instrumental music, with the exception of operas, musical plays, and large choral works.

Any composer who has published music, or whose
compositions are frequently performed in public,
should apply to the Secretary for details of membership. There is no entrance fee or subscription; the
present membership is over five thousand.

Songwriters' Guild of Great Britain

The purpose of this body, whose membership
includes most authors and composers of light music and
songs, is to secure better representation, and fair publishing terms, for writers of British popular music. It
also offers expert advice and help to its members on
legal and business matters. Details of membership
may be obtained from the General Secretary, 32 Shaftes-
bury Avenue, London W.1.

Composers' Guild of Great Britain

The function of this Guild (10 Stratford Place,
London W.1.) is to protect the interest of composer
members (mostly of serious music) in this country, and
to offer them any advice and assistance that they may
need.

Mechanical Copyright Protection Society

This organization undertakes the collection and
distribution of fees for the mechanical reproduction of
music and songs, on records, tapes, etc. The writer's
share of mechanical fees may be paid to him either by
his publisher, or (by arrangement) direct from Mechani-

cal Copyright Protection Society Ltd., 380 Streatham High Road, London S.W.16.

The Light Music Society

This Society was founded to further the cause of light music. The membership includes both professional composers and others who are interested in light music. As well as sponsoring concerts and records, the Society holds periodic meetings, and arranges competitions for non-professional composers; these serve the very useful purpose of enabling successful competitors to hear their music performed and, in some cases, broadcast. The Society also sponsors competitions for professional composers. Details of membership may be obtained from the Secretary, Mrs. Levan, 17 Bushwood Road, Kew Green, Richmond, Surrey, TW9 3BG.

Opportunities for Composers

A composer cannot afford to neglect any opportunity of hearing his music played, or of getting it published, recorded, or broadcast.

From time to time, competitions are arranged by various organizations which offer prizes (and, more important, performances) to successful candidates. Details of these competitions may be found in journals such as *The Musical Times*. Contests organized by television companies (e.g. for new Christmas Carols) are also of considerable importance, since success could lead to wide publicity.

A composer with a flair for descriptive incidental music might possibly find an opening with one of the publishers who have libraries of background (or mood) music, used for television, films, etc. It is difficult to break into this field, however, though the rewards for success may be considerable.

SOME USEFUL BOOKS

COLE, WILLIAM. *The Form of Music* (Associated Board (1969).

DEMUTH, NORMAN. *A Course in Musical Composition* (Bosworth, 4 vols., 1950).

HINDEMITH, PAUL. *The Craft of Musical Composition* (Schott, 2 vols., 1958).

HUTCHINGS, ARTHUR. *The Invention and Composition of Music* (Novello, 1958).

KITSON, C. H. *Elementary Harmony* (Oxford University Press, 1926).

—— *The Elements of Musical Composition* (Oxford University Press, 1936).

—— *The Evolution of Harmony* (Oxford University Press, 1924).

LINDSAY, MARTIN. *Songwriting* (Teach Yourself Books, 1955).

PALMER, KING. *Music* (Teach Yourself Books, 1944).

INDEX